Qualitative Inquiry: Critical Ethics, Justice, and Activism Series
Gaile S. Cannella, Editor

The **Qualitative Inquiry: Critical Ethics, Justice, and Activism** series is a collection designed to provide a cross-disciplinary overview of the use of qualitative research as an avenue for justice and critical transformative activism/action socially, environmentally, and related to more-than-human/human entanglements. Much of this work has been/is labeled critical qualitative research. Scholarship that addresses the complexities of ethico/onto/epistemological orientations in critical work is included, as well as both the diverse critical histories (e.g. feminisms, post-colonial/indigenous, poststructuralist) and contemporary becomings (e.g. counter neoliberal, decolonial, beyond human) that currently, and may in the future, unveil(s) power complexities and performances in ways that move toward more just transformations. Authors are invited to submit manuscripts focusing on the basics necessary for conducting critical transformative qualitative inquiry, contemporary views and conceptualizations of critique, critical research as direct activism, and critical scholarship that thinks research differently. Further, philosophies, traditionally unthought methodologies (e.g. counter and/or multispecies ethnography, diffraction), digital and media technologies as data and/or method in critical qualitative inquiry, methodologies usually labeled traditional that have been reconceptualized and employed for critical purposes, disruptive methodologies, and complexity methodologies like assemblage theories are encouraged.

Books in the Series–
Making Research Public in Troubled Times by M. Francyne Huckaby (2018)
Researching Resistance by M. Francyne Huckaby (2019)
Employing Critical Qualitative Inquiry to Mount Nonviolent Resistance by Yvonna S. Lincoln and Gaile S. Cannella (2019)
Exploring Data Production in Motion by Teija Rantala (forthcoming)

Gaile S. Canella (EdD, University of Georgia) is an independent scholar who has served as a tenured Full Professor at Texas A&M University – College Station and at Arizona State University – Tempe, as well as the Velma Schmidt Endowed Chair of Education at the University of North Texas. The editor of the Qualitative Inquiry: Critical Ethics, Justice, and Activism series is interested in reviewing manuscripts and proposals for possible publication in the series. Scholars who wish to be considered should email their proposals, along with two sample chapters and current CVs, to the editors. For instructions and advice on preparing a prospectus, please refer to the Myers Education Press website at http://myersedpress.com/sites/stylus/MEP/Docs/Prospectus%20Guidelines%20MEP.pdf. You can send your material to:

Gaile S. Cannella
gaile.cannella@gmail.com

Employing Critical Qualitative Inquiry to Mount Nonviolent Resistance

Employing Critical Qualitative Inquiry to Mount Nonviolent Resistance

EDITED BY
Yvonna S. Lincoln and Gaile S. Cannella

FEATURING
M. Francyne Huckaby, Valerie Kinloch, and Janet L. Miller

Gorham, Maine

Copyright © 2019 | Myers Education Press, LLC

Published by Myers Education Press, LLC
P.O. Box 424 Gorham, ME 04038

All rights reserved. No part of this book may be reprinted or reproduced in any form or by any electronic, mechanical, or other means, now known or hereafter invented, including photocopying, recording, and information storage and retrieval, without permission in writing from the publisher.

Myers Education Press is an academic publisher specializing in books, e-books and digital content in the field of education. All of our books are subjected to a rigorous peer review process and produced in compliance with the standards of the Council on Library and Information Resources.

LIBRARY OF CONGRESS CATALOGING-IN-PUBLICATION DATA AVAILABLE FROM LIBRARY OF CONGRESS.

13-digit ISBN 978-1-9755-0044-3 (paperback)
13-digit ISBN 978-1-9755-0043-6 (hard cover)
13-digit ISBN 978-1-9755-0045-0 (library networkable e-edition)
13-digit ISBN 978-1-9755-0046-7 (consumer e-edition)

Printed in the United States of America.

All first editions printed on acid-free paper that meets the American National Standards Institute Z39-48 standard.

Books published by Myers Education Press may be purchased at special quantity discount rates for groups, workshops, training organizations and classroom usage. Please call our customer service department at 1-800-232-0223 for details.

Cover design by Sophie Appel

Visit us on the web at www.myersedpress.com to browse our complete list of titles.

Table of Contents

1. Research and Struggles in the Contemporary Political World   1
   Gaile S. Cannella and Yvonna S. Lincoln

2. Difficult Love: Preparations of a Warrior   25
   M. Francyne Huckaby

3. "Unbought and Unbossed": On Being Black, Woman, and Transgressive in the Fight for Justice   43
   Valerie Kinloch

4. Sanity on the Chopping Block, or How to Save Yourself in an Insane World   57
   Yvonna S. Lincoln

5. Shuffling the Deck: The "Woman Card," Misogyny, and Material-Discursive Complexities of "Identities"   71
   Janet L. Miller

6. Resisting Patriarchy: Explorations Using a Collaborative Protest Play   97
   Gaile S. Cannella

7. Resources for Becomingswith Activism, Research, and Contemporary Politics   115
   Gaile S. Cannella and Yvonna S. Lincoln

   Editors & Contributors   125

CHAPTER ONE

Research and Struggles in the Contemporary Political World

Gaile S. Cannella
Yvonna S. Lincoln

> Nonviolence means avoiding not only external physical violence but also internal violence of spirit. You not only refuse to shoot a man, but you refuse to hate him. (King, 2003, p. 453)

SO MANY OF us (in the United States, but potentially around the globe) were disappointed and distressed by the conduct of the 2016 U.S. presidential election. The results dashed our hopes that misogyny, racism, capitalist patriarchy, even speciesism and capitalist destruction of the earth, as well as so many other forms of disqualification, violence, and erasure had been, at least, acknowledged as injustices in the public imaginary (even if not always addressed). Feminist, poststructural, postcolonial, and other forms of critical research, as well as all manner of diverse voices and ways of being, have demonstrated that democratic society in general, and educational practices specifically, are dependent on respect for the complexities, becomings-with, and multiplicities of all manner of earth critters ("becoming-with" and "critters" used by Donna Haraway, 2015), whether human or more-than-human. More importantly, justice for all requires safety, support, being valued, equity, fairness, and opportunity in equal measure. However, even as so many critical scholars from diverse fields and perspectives have spent their lives supporting multiple knowledges and challenging injustice, the power of patriarchal capitalism has remained a major force for marginalization, inequity, the perpetuation of intersectional oppressions, and even violence.

Appropriately labeled by bell hooks (2001) as "white supremacist capitalist patriarchy," in the current condition, we ask ourselves as human beings, educators, and researchers: What do we do next? How do we deal with our feelings? our despair? After years of work toward justice and equity, are there ways we can counter this patriarchal, capitalist whitelash in our daily lives? Before organizing this volume, and in our despair related to the 2016 election, we as panel members and additional participant scholars came together at two conferences to demonstrate personal actions taken by researchers to deal with thoughts/feelings that we hoped would help us move toward survival. We wanted to generate rethought, and even new, research methodologies (frameworks) as counter measures. Early on, some scholars turned down our invitations to participate, saying involvement would be even more upsetting. However, we continued and presented papers, conducted protest performances with our audiences, and completed coalition-building activities. We believe that our ethical responsibilities are to continue to research, to go public, and to take action.

The 2016 election in the United States reminded us that intersecting oppressions and injustices are alive and well in societies broadly, whether locally or globally. Critical scholars and public activists in a range of fields and from diverse ethnic, gender, and racial locations have inquired into and challenged these power plays and hegemonic assemblages for years (Bordo, 2017a)—as examples, from the actions of Sojourner Truth to Kimberle Crenshaw on intersectionality (1989). There exist multiple literatures and forms of public and community activisms and resistance historically confronting patriarchy, racism, misogyny, and the destruction imposed through various forms of injustice and oppression. We believe that we should acknowledge and engage with this resistance history and presence.

However, we would also recognize that this research and multiple performances of public activism have not always been followed by transformations toward a more just world (Cannella & Lincoln, 2009). Further, critical researchers face accusations of academic elitism (Latour, 2004) and activists are often accused of playing identity politics (Lilla, 2016), just to name a few examples of the oversimplified forms of disqualification used to discredit and silence. Further, current theoretical perspectives offer opportunities for recognizing the privileged role of "human beings" in the literal construction of injustice, damage, and destruction (e.g., the Anthropocene); yet, blaming all "human beings" for privilege "over" other humans (e.g., women;

People of Color; those labeled as poor, persons with disabilities, non-English speaking people) or other living beings (e.g., other animals, plants, the Earth) is problematic. This imposition of a universal human culpability denies the ultimate and continued intersecting, rhyzomatic, and intertwined roles of patriarchy (von Werlhof, 2007; Lerner, 1986) and capitalism (the Capitalocene, Moore, 2016, 2015), along with specific groups of human beings, in the origins, continuation, and reinscriptions of sexism, racism, and yes, even speciesism, environmental destruction, and all manner of injustice.

As we have all become aware, power inequities are played out in all aspects of society. One major example is public education, with impositions of injustice and inequity ranging from privatization that limits access, to curriculum that would control, to beliefs in evaluation that would judge, label, and limit—and on and on. To support public education that provides equal access and opportunity for all, education researchers and other scholars must engage themselves with these issues broadly, as they are also played out in other aspects of society. Patriarchal and capitalist impositions and damage are infused throughout areas like health care, living conditions, and equal access broadly defined, in environmental damage, and in the lack of environmental justice, just to name a few. As has been explained from a range of perspectives, neoliberalism (Foucault, 2008), or so-called capitalist patriarchy (von Werlhof, 2007), has become rhizomatically attached to, and envelops, all aspects of our existence. Whether labeled human animals or nonhuman animals, environment or place, value is now imposed through capitalism, an all-invasive capitalism that is always and already marked by misogyny, sexism, and racism.

We could continue with multiple daily examples under the Trump administration in the United States. Again to illustrate briefly, as we began writing this chapter, the Trump administration (in existence for 16–18 months at the time of these actions) had separated children from their parents as they attempted to cross the southern border of the United States to escape rape, torture, gang violence, and murder in their homelands. Based on the little information that could be gathered—as reporters and even members of Congress were barred from most forms of access—the separation was achieved by placing adults and children into large, seven- to eight-foot-high cages in different locations. Many in the United States (and around the globe) were and are extremely concerned about what was happening to these children as they were ripped away from their parents and the ways this will forever negatively affect their lives. Obviously, injustice is being perpetrated overall on this group of families, adults, and children of color. Marches have occurred; civil rights lawyers and other advocates have traveled to the southern border and other locations as they have determined where children were taken. A judge has ordered that the separated families be reunited. Yet within this administratively constructed disaster, many wonder if some of the children will ever be reunited with their parents. These are such difficult times that it has never been more important to stand for justice, and this is just one more horrific example. In these times, we as scholars must literally take a stance for justice in the research that we choose to conduct.

To illustrate a stance that would employ research as nonviolent resistance, in this volume five different authors demonstrate differing forms of critical qualitative inquiry employed as counteractivity in reaction to the 2016 U.S. presidential election and the continued daily incompetence and horrific actions exhibited by the administration since its inauguration in January 2017. In their chapters, the researchers demonstrate how current methods like autoethnography, historical analysis, and juxtaposition can be used for critical inquiry, survival, and public action during difficult times. Further, some scholars insist that reconceptualized problems and methods are needed, as well as perspectives and intersectional forms of inquiry that address justice, equity, and privilege more inclusively. Finally, more public dissemination methods, like performance and arts-based work, are demonstrated as researchers are encouraged to share, collaborate, and act with/and in communities. Since higher education is conceptualized as a learning environment, scholars do tend to have more freedom than most workers. For this reason, and because justice and equity have never been more important than they are in today's backward-leaning environment, critical scholars must become even more political and action oriented in their research.

Positioning Critical Qualitative Researchers

As the editors and lead authors of the volume, we want to begin by positioning ourselves as critical qualitative scholars and teachers who continue to struggle with the notion of research broadly as always and already a power construct and an often elitist, colonialist practice. Yet, we also continue to believe that since so-called (by the dominant North and West) human beings have historically chosen to act and continue to perpetuate the research construct, whether well intended or not, we must become more responsible for those actions and our research conceptualizations, as well as less centered on our privileged, White selves. As we choose to act through inquiry, publications, pedagogy, and community work, there are worries within which we (and some others) continue to struggle. This list of worries is not complete, but we hope that it is at least thought provoking for the reader who would hope to conduct critical qualitative research in difficult political times.

- Research as construct is problematic from any perspective. Many of us have critiqued the Enlightenment/modernist creation for most of our professional lives, asking questions like: How can anyone have the right to speak for, interpret, or represent "others"? How does one deal with the power hierarchy that is intrinsic to a construct like research, because the construct will likely not be eliminated in the science-oriented, deterministic world in which we must survive? As "trained" researchers, what are our ethical responsibilities within this context?

- We live in a time that would deny our interconnected histories, treating everyone as entrepreneurs of their own thoughts, as "new" knowledge creators. Yet, there is likely no author (Barthes, 2002; Derrida, 1978; Foucault, 1977), no researcher, writer, or scholar who is independent of the many academic, community, or cultural ancestors who have gone before. How do we always and already make these historical acknowledgements while at the same time challenging dominant academic, western pressures to "know all the literature" or "be the expert"?

- Language and thinking almost always oversimplify. Whatever we think, act, or become is usually reified at the performance, the interpretation, or even throughout the becoming. As teachers and scholars, how do we think, perform, engage, and interact with complex, contradictory ideas and relations while making informed introductions of those ideas to new scholars and other students and readers? How do I/we respectfully engage the scholarship and actions of critical justice ancestors without perpetuating positivist, colonialist privileging? As Lorde (2007) reminds us regarding the master's tools: If a researcher has been conventionally placed in the margin (e.g., through race, gender, even academic background), how much of the dominant must be considered, while in the end eliminated, in order to transform and decenter?

- Critical work has not always been successful. Currently, some scholars invoke Latour (2004), as he has labeled critical scholarship as not transformative, as elitist, as "running out of steam." We disagree and feel that both academia and society more broadly exhibit a range of critical transformations that have been facilitated through critical qualitative inquiry. Further, we feel that a simplistic critique of past critical work, as currently accepted and used by some, itself perpetuates dualisms (e.g., in the use of affirmation or negation), Enlightenment linear views of academic and social progress, oversimplifications, denial of diverse cultural conceptualizations, and human privilege that, in our understandings, the "critique of critique" would have hoped to counter (Ray & Selinger, 2008; Noys, 2011; Folkers, 2016). While attempting to always question and critique ourselves, we think of critical work in a Foucauldian genealogical sense, which means going beyond the more structuralist perspective related to how facts become matters of concern (as examined in Foucault's *The Archeology of Knowledge*, 1972), to question if certain matters should be of concern. Further, we remind ourselves that critical investigations can be considered events that themselves actually become ways to limit the power of dominant forms of reason (Foucault, 1997; Folkers, 2016). So, how do we continue to construct inquiry that challenges, limits, and transforms domination?

- Research has tended to be for and about those who have labeled themselves "human." Yet, to be critical, inquiry should also question the notion that human privilege is always more important than justice for other living creatures and/or the environment. Further, will we ever attain justice—socially or otherwise—for all "humans" if human beings are always considered most important? We have tended to speak of justice and equity in human social terms, while at the same time many of us who are labeled "human" have not been treated fairly. These unjustly treated human beings have been labeled *animal, savage,* and *childlike* (thereby also creating the categories of nonhumans, People of Color, and those who are younger, who are "less than" particular groups of "human beings"). We have never achieved social justice or socioeconomic equity for all human beings and should continue to place social fairness and equity at the forefront. However, as critical scholars we do struggle with this continued human privilege. We are beginning to ask: What does justice mean for the more-than-human, for living beings who have not had the privileged human voice? What does justice mean for the Earth? Can justice and equity, social and otherwise, ever be attained as long as those who have labeled themselves *human* (and controlled the label) construct the definitions and circumstances in which all others, human or otherwise, must survive?

- We (and maybe all of us) continue to struggle with our own understandings, beliefs, and experiences. These internal confusions surround our interpretations of the thoughts, work, and actions of others, whether so-called human or more-than-human others. So we ask the very personal questions: Am I humble enough to listen and listen again, to read as much as I should read, to humbly attempt to engage with past and present ideas and scholarship, to work hard to understand and construct possibilities, to turn my world upside-down? Can I take risks regarding my own interpretations while always challenging those interpretations? How do I continue to perpetuate a critical justice research agenda without claiming new power for myself?

Obviously, we are concerned about justice and equity in all forms, but we do not have profound insights for addressing these concerns. Rather, we hope that we (and other critical researchers) embody a continued critical awareness. From within this standpoint, we want to introduce our interpretations of critical research, an understanding embedded within qualitative research/inquiry, diverse histories, and a multiplicity of philosophies. First, we briefly summarize our understandings specifically related to beliefs about reality and knowledge as research constructs. Then, critical qualitative research is overviewed more fully. Finally, we provide an overview of each chapter.

Exploring Research Ontologies, Histories, and Entanglements

As researchers, we have come to a point in which we understand research as multiple, historical, fluid, complex, constructed, and always necessarily interrogated and multiple (Koro-Ljungberg, 2016), often prescriptively undefinable. To have a feel for this multiplicity, researchers must explore the notion of inquiry as a construct and practice not only historically and philosophically, but most importantly, ontologically. Much has been written on the history of research or inquiry and associated concepts like theory, research questions, design, data, analysis, results, and paradigm. Historically, the Enlightenment/modernist embeddedness of research has been accepted in one form or another, whether as (a) scientific inquiry that would, at least partially, uncover reality (most often labeled postpositivist, critical realist, or the scientific method) or, as (b) postmodern emergent, empirical contingencies always/already generated through researcher interactive constructions and intersections with participants, institutions, material relations, or life worlds, often with an underlying concern for power, equity, and justice. Research that is concerned with power and equity has been labeled everything from *critical* to *poststructural* to *endarkened feminist* to *postqualitative* to *posthuman*—and all kinds of ontological and epistemological perspectives, relations, and worldviews in between. These concerns with power originate from diverse locations and have often refused to ally; however, whether connected or not, each has, in one way or another, attempted to address unequal and unjust power relations.

As is hopefully implied by the naming of these two broad-based perspectives, research as construct and practice can be understood as ontological, representing the scholar's beliefs about reality and the nature of being, whether acknowledged or not by the researcher. Further, research is a philosophical performance, even though not always recognized or identified by the researcher. A range of philosophical perspectives, underpinnings, and histories are entangled to form various research foundations.

Additionally, to broadly discuss research/inquiry as a construct that is conceptualized from a wide range of ontological and philosophical positions, in this volume we use the field labeled *qualitative research* because the practices in the field represent diversity across disciplines as well as ontological perspectives that range from postpositivist theory building to inquiry that would attempt to recenter the marginalized. We do not use *quantitative research* here—inquiry that tends to privilege descriptive and/or inferential numerical methodologies—because most forms are embedded within conventional ontological belief structures. These ontological perspectives do not question the existence of universal reality that can be at least approximated using quantitative measurements (operationalized as representing that reality) and statistical analysis that would reveal probable "truths" regarding that reality. Quantitative research therefore represents much narrower—and more deterministic—ontological approaches to inquiry. Although many researchers continue to privilege quantitative research conceptualizations and practices, qualitative inquiry allows for almost limitless approaches to ontology, philosophy, and practice, providing for more complete understandings of the range of research histories and locations. The field of qualitative inquiry has been/is the ideal diffractive location from which critical inquiry broadly can be conceptualized and practiced.

In *The Paradigm Dialog* (1990), Egon Guba reminded us that ontological and philosophical responses regarding research are the starting points for inquiry, whether actively considered by the researcher or not. The basic philosophical questions that ground research—again, whether acknowledged or denied—are the following (statements from Guba, 1990, p. 18, in quotes, with our additional questions added as related to power):

1. "Ontological: What is the nature of the 'knowable'? Or, what is the nature of 'reality'?" What are purposes and conceptualizations of research within diverse views of reality? Existence? Being? Is ontological perspective ever an ethical issue? How, when, and why? How does the construction of the ontological question represent human privilege? Can research be conceptualized without this concern for being, existence, or reality? What does this mean for justice and equity?

2. "Epistemological: What is the nature of the relationship between the knower (the inquirer) and the known (or knowable)?" Do particular relationships or conceptualizations create privilege and/or power for the inquirer? How do various stakeholder positions influence the knowable? Who and what is included? Who decides what is included? Who has no say over what is included?

3. "Methodological: How should the inquirer go about finding out knowledge?" How does ontology influence/construct/becomewith methodology and the knowledge that emerges? How is methodology a facilitative construct, and what is facilitated? How does methodology inhibit?

In one way or another, the diverse perspectives on research have either incorporated these questions or generated additional questions that are ontological, epistemological, and methodological. The reader will note that our issues at the beginning of the chapter can all be considered ontological, epistemological, and methodological. Additionally, we have always considered the issues to be ethical, not as a predetermined ethics, but rather as underlying values and emergent unpredictable concerns (Cannella & Lincoln, 2011) and believe that for many scholars a fourth category, ethical consideration, is not only necessary (Barad, 2007), but has been a concern for a number of years. Further, most recently, and expressed in our list of critical concerns, some scholars in the social sciences have stressed that research as construct has privileged and exceptionalized human beings as the center of everything, and that research is an anthropocentric practice that marginalizes, silences, even erases other living beings, the material world, and even the complex entanglements within and across. For research, these concerns are referred to as *postanthropocentric* or *posthuman inquiry* and can lead to expansion, or even elimination, of ontological, epistemological, and methodological questions. After all, if the human is decentered, what happens to human constructions like *truth/reality, knowing, method, research,* and *data*? However, others have reminded researchers that the "centered human" has consistently been defined as White, male, and Euro-American, and that there are "people" who have never been at the center (Jackson, 2015). These become very complex, entangled, ethical issues regarding research conceptualizations, decisions, and practices.

Importantly, the reader will note that from most perspectives, with the exception of postpositivism, the ontological and epistemological separation/distinction is "obliterated" (Guba, 1990, p. 27). Further, for 25–30 years, philosophical perspectives related to research have, to a major extent, entangled reality with the researcher, thus "'producing'" notions of inquiry as emergent, relational, even becoming, and therefore always and already some form of ethical stance, whether acknowledged or not.

From this broad-based introduction, we hope that the reader will now join us as we move to a brief historical comparison of research as conceptualized to approximate a universal reality, most often referred to as postpositivism, with research conceptualized from within the multiple postmodern challenges to universal realities/truth. What/who/how is research from within each viewed?

Postpositivism: Inquiry as Objective Approximation of Reality

Conventional inquiry/research is most often labeled *postpositivism*. Ontologically, while reality is put forward as never fully understood or truth as completely revealed (and positivism would literally find the truth), the existence of reality is accepted and is considered evidenced through natural laws and universals. Data in conventional research is, at times, literally believed to consist of minor performances of these natural laws and universals. Further, objectivity in the pursuit of information and the analysis of that information regulates the extent to which reality (truth, knowledge) can be approximated. Further, the researcher is considered independent from the reality that is studied (and revealed) and the data that are collected and analyzed. The researcher is judged by accuracy of representation and the efficiency in which theory, method, data collection, and analysis are conceptualized and practiced. Focusing here on qualitative research (as the best form of inquiry that explains diverse perspectives), methodologies range from verification of theoretical ideas through data collection, to discovery of "knowledge" through practices like qualitative research in natural settings that is considered to yield grounded theories.

Postpositivism accepts and perpetuates the research construct as progressive, positive, and leading to scientific change if followed systematically and objectively. Components like theory, research questions, design, data collection and analysis, and results originated (and are not questioned if practiced rigorously) within this positivist/postpositivist belief structure.

Some forms of inquiry, usually labeled critical realism, can also be considered postpositivist and conventional. Similar to more-open belief structures, critical realist views acknowledge that the researcher's subjective values are always part of inquiry and will even ask questions like: What values and whose values are governing the research? This incorporation of researcher values introduces the idea that inquiry is a political act. However, critical realism ultimately accepts the notion that reality exists and can at least be approximated, however political its description by a particular researcher. Therefore, to conduct "'good'" critical realist inquiry, one must create ways of being as objective as possible to gather the most accurate data possible, and to ultimately approximate reality as closely as possible.

Postpositivist qualitative research is most often associated with data collection methods like observations, interviews (including researcher transcripts, audiotapes, and videotapes, practices like focus groups), and collections of artifacts and texts (e.g., objects and documents). From within a research design that is either predetermined or flexibly emergent, the information is viewed as requiring that the researcher be as accurate as is humanly possible. Ethnography, case study, and approaches like discourse analysis are example forms of representation that have been developed by combining these basic data collection methods and have literally dominated the construction of fields like anthropology and played major roles in fields like sociology, communication studies, education, and linguistics.

Grounded theory (Glaser & Strauss, 1967) is probably the most commonly referenced systematic approach to postpositivist qualitative research. The practice was created as a reaction to the absolute truth orientations found in positivism that begin with theory, and it follows with qualitative data collection designed to reveal, and prove, the "truth" or "reality" of the theory. Basically, grounded theory turns the process upside-down and is a data-driven process; the notion is that theory follows data, rather than preceding data. Theory as a construct that would explain universal truths is accepted; however, data are the foundation for theory development rather than vice versa. Strauss and Corbin (1994) describe grounded theory as "a way of thinking about and conceptualizing data" (p. 275). Further, the description of grounded theory put forward the notion of constant comparative analysis, a method for seeing and manipulating data. The researcher moves back and forth between data collection and analysis, determining what further data are needed, additional analysis, back and forth until the researcher believes that data saturation is achieved as data will begin to repeat themselves. Grounded theory also introduces the practice of coding, a practice through which the researcher divides the data into related categories or themes. While data-coding procedures (which will not be discussed here) can be standardized to varying degrees and complexities and are expected to be rigorous, postpositivist perspectives also insist that coding protects the researcher from biases that would privilege particular voices over others in the common context of qualitative research that is almost always multiple. Some would consider the postpositivist research process to be all about data, either as discovery or proof—data that in one way or another represents, and may actually be, reality.

Qualitative research does not always look the same, even in postpositivism. For example, in the traditional period of the early 20th century, researchers were to collect data that represented the alien "other" objectively, validly, and reliably, and assumed the researcher's right and power to represent stories of others. During a more modernist period in the middle of the 20th century, postpositivist work was more formalized as graduate students and scholars were "drawn to qualitative research practices that would let them (*as the researcher*) give voice to society's underclass" (Denzin & Lincoln, 1998, p. 16, emphasis added) as with critical realism. Not only do these views remain, but contemporarily, with the use of computer-assisted storehouses for data, calls are made for large qualitative data bases, qualitative data mining, integrating qualitative data bases, and qualitative data warehousing. Postpositivist qualitative research is growing by leaps and bounds, especially as technology has made possible massive storage and the expansion of all kinds of analyses, from thematic approaches, to word groupings, to rhetorical reactions, to combinations of text with video, and on and on. The basic assumptions regarding research, data, and researcher, especially ontologically and epistemologically, remain the same. Research is to approximate reality as closely as possible; increased justice and equity are not ultimately placed at the forefront.

Further, within a modernist, capitalist context, a reinvigorated belief in close approximations to reality and standardization of data and methods are again (or have always been) dominant. Postpositivist qualitative research broadly is an ideal capitalist territory with lines of flight that continue to circle back to capitalism through commodification of so-called new knowledges, marketed coding technologies, textbook and computer analysis software sales, and entrepreneurial qualitative researcher experts who sell their services (Deleuze & Guattari, 1987; Cannella & Koro-Ljungberg, 2017; Koro-Ljungberg & Cannella, 2018). Postpositivism broadly is not a critical practice.

Postmodern Upheavals: Inquiry as Challenging Deterministic Universals

Many would insist (and probably accurately) that postpositivism continues to dominate the research community for a range of reasons that include a modernist, capitalist context. However, as truth-oriented research perspectives and practices have developed, many have disagreed with such belief systems, arguing that the complexity of life and difference must be at the forefront, arguing that ontological and epistemological questions must be acknowledged. Developing out of a range of fields like philosophy, literature, and art, along with academic disciplines, the belief in predetermined reality or truth has therefore been increasingly challenged in a variety of ways. Additionally, embedded within the diverse philosophies (and fields) that have questioned the existence of predetermined truths is the notion that human beings create these realities (social constructions of meaning) from within their own lived conditions (physical, cultural, individual), as well as belief structures and biases (Lincoln & Guba, 1985: see Chapter 3, "Constructed Realities").

Yet, postpositivist, modernist perspectives and belief in universal truths remain so dominant that some readers may not be familiar with critiques of this philosophical value system. Even though originating from diverse philosophical and life locations, the challenges are often (although oversimplified) labeled postmodernism. The work of Lyotard (1984) in *The Postmodern Condition: A Report on Knowledge* illustrates these revolutionary challenges most clearly. Lyotard problematizes the ontological belief in predetermined truth using concepts like *regimes of truth* and *grand narratives*. Dominant Western beliefs are put forward as realities (regimes of truth) and supported by grand narratives that privilege ways of thinking, speaking, and being that are consistent with the truth regime. An example (among many providesd by Lyotard) is the discourse on reason and education that would deliver the poor from ignorance and servitude, a grand narrative that silences the economic and institutional inequities that deny opportunity and diversity and chain particular groups and individuals to oppressive life conditions. For the past 30–40 years, postmodern perspectives have critiqued modernist beliefs in preexisting structures and universal truths like linearity, predetermined outcomes, and dualistic thought ranging from adult/child, male/female, Black/White, objective/subjective to right/wrong, nature/culture, mind/body (Fleck, 1979; Cooper & Burrell, 1988; Denzin, 1991; Seidman, 1994).

Justice and the Multiplicities of Critical Research

As a greater range of human voices has been acknowledged following attempts to achieve equitable environments and opportunities like civil rights and social justice broadly, the multiplicities of life experiences and ways of understanding, even constructing the world, have been increasingly heard and acknowledged. People on the streets and in their own communities, activists, and researchers have been concerned with the social injustices and inequities that are experienced by individual human beings and groups in all types of locations around the globe. Scholars with these concerns would address power in all its multiple complexities and performances, but continue to challenge truth orientations of any type (even while attempting to avoid power as a deterministic truth). The theoretical perspectives are also multiple and include poststructuralism, critical pedagogy, a range of feminisms, queer theory, and currently posthuman perspectives, as well as indigenous/postcolonial/subaltern ways of being, just to name a few (Cannella, 2015). In 1994, Kincheloe and McLaren described "a criticalist as a researcher or theorist who attempts to use her or his work as a form of social or cultural criticism" (p. 139) and is concerned about power relations, fluidity, oppression, and privilege. Further, postmodern critical scholars tend to believe that research has been, and is, a construct that facilitates and reproduces oppression. Embedded within these concerns are, therefore, the beliefs that research is always an ethical encounter, that the researcher should always/already avoid the construction of power for self, and that scholarship should promote justice and equity.

Although there is a range of philosophical views within concern for power and justice, postmodern critical perspectives tend to accept ethico-onto-epistemological beliefs that would challenge predetermined universal truths. Reality and the knower are not separate, and justice and equity (in some form) are certainly the agendas. For example, while postcolonial scholars would problematize continued colonialism, the focus would actually be the multiplicities and indeterminacies of the colonial present as well as diverse knowledges and interpretations that would challenge colonizer ways of being. Rather than determining exact colonial truth or perpetuating colonizer/colonized dualisms within which the colonized become the powerful (thus dominating or controlling the colonizer), the agenda is transformation toward a more just world for all. Additionally, the expressed belief in contingency, researcher interpretations that will always and already be subjective, multiplicity along with fluidity, and scholarly attempts to avoid further impositions of power that are always embedded within research as construct are present in some form in the various constructions of critical inquiry.

Critical scholarship attempts to reveal the hidden workings of power, examining language use and the circulation of discourses as power is facilitated. Discourses are also understood as including artifacts, practices, thoughts, forms of representation and actions, as well as what can and cannot be said. Traditionally, critical research/inquiry has been associated with concern for justice in the social sciences as it relates to issues of race, gender, socioeconomic level, and other intersecting and reified forms of oppression and inequity. Increasingly, scholars have expressed concern that this research has not been transformative, has not led to increased social justice. So, issues of transformation have become prominent. Additionally, and perhaps more "radically," as mentioned previously, some critical scholars have pointed to the human centeredness of research, that relations are denied, that materialities are ignored, and that the nonhuman is erased or placed in the service of the human.

These are the broad-based, postmodern conceptualizations of critical research that include concerns about justice and equity in all forms, and range from (but are not limited to) poststructural genealogical interventions—to diverse feminisms, including new materialisms—to queer theory—to critical race theory—to postcolonial/subaltern/ indigenous perspectives—to the more narrow, fairly modernist conceptualizations of critical that are embedded within the Frankfurt School construction of Critical Theory—to Freirean critical pedagogy—to diverse conceptualizations of what is contemporarily referred to as posthumanism. Some refer to critical qualitative research as literally "stemming from critical theory" (Steinberg, 2012, p. ix). While always avoiding a unitary conceptualization, others believe that a more complete concern for justice and equity requires the inclusion of the multiple perspectives, lives, histories, and voices that may often not be labeled critical.

Further, for over 30 years, calls have been made for a critical social science (Popkewitz, 1990) or a form of anticolonial science (Rau, 2005). Further—with recent recognition that justice broadly is of concern, especially regarding the environment, the Earth, and beings that have not been labeled human, along with the recognition that human relationships are not just social—perhaps concern for only the social should be understood as improperly limiting our justice agenda. Therefore, we choose to use the term *critical qualitative science/inquiry* here as a broad-based concept that represents the mass of lives, ways of being, environment, multiplicities, and academic literatures that have faced, and continue to deal with, oppression, injustice, marginalization, even silencing and erasure (e.g., extinction). We use the term *critical* here, but totally understand that others may prefer labels like *anticolonial* (Rau, 2005; Cannella & Manuelito, 2008), or even just *research* (Fine, 2018). We attempt here to use critical as an all-inclusive, fluid, yet diffractive (Haraway, 2000, p. 104; Barad, 2007, p. 90) location from which transformative justice and equity can be addressed.

Even during these political times that are difficult, depressing, even violent, the diffractive, nonviolent possibilities embedded within conceptualizations of critical research are unlimited as sites for justice and transformation. Further, however risks may be perceived, researchers remain in fairly privileged and safe positions from which they can do their work. Therefore, we use this volume to demonstrate the multidirectional, nonviolent resistance research generated by scholars related to the current Trump administration. Five examples are provided that include: autoethnography of survival; historical examination of Black activism; reconceptualized research problems, both traditionally and from a feminist poststructural perspective; and performance as research.

Surviving and Countering Patriarchal Whitelash: Resistance Research by "Nasty Women"

Along with many others, we female educators and researchers were, through our politically activist sister Hillary Rodham Clinton, referred to as "Nasty Women" in the U.S. presidential debates. We therefore organized researcher "Nasty Women" sessions at both the International Congress of Qualitative Inquiry in 2017 and the American Educational Research Association conference in 2018. Through our research and actions for and in these sessions, we hoped to generate nonviolent forms of resistance that would become ways of being, thinking, and acting as scholars in our current unjust political circumstance. Living and working contemporarily, we ask ourselves as human beings, educators, and researchers: What do we do next? How do we deal with our feelings?

Our despair? After years of work toward justice and equity, are there ways we can counter this patriarchal, capitalist whitelash in our daily lives? As educators? As researchers? As citizens? Perhaps this particular difficult circumstance can be the point from which we can demonstrate the multiplicities and unlimited possibilities for employing critical qualitative research as survival tool, as counteraction, and as instrument for more just reconceptualizations and transformations.

The broad purposes of the chapters in this book are, therefore, (1) to demonstrate personal actions taken by researchers to help them deal with thoughts/feelings and to move toward survival, as well as (2) to illustrate new and rethought research methodologies (frameworks) as countermeasures, as nonviolent forms of resistance. The final chapter in the volume serves as a reference for all those scholars hoping to explore and learn more, as well as to take direct action. In difficult political, social, and environmental circumstances, critical qualitative research is of utmost importance. The following is a brief introduction to our featured researchers.

Chapter Two is an autobiographical inquiry titled "Difficult Love: Preparations of a Warrior." M. Francyne Huckaby explores how she prepared herself for the upcoming wars imposed by a potential Donald Trump victory—wars that would be figurative, literal, and political—on women, between nation-states, and among Americans themselves, from the North, the South, and the Center. She resurrects familial memories of war—World War II, Korea, and Vietnam. In preparation for the losses of war, she explains how she retreated to the darkness of dreams, meditation, and memory, as well as conversation with family members to steel herself for the blows to come, as well as the mounting of resistance. Difficult questions are posed, like: How should one live? What kind of life is worth living? What risks are worth taking? Turning to Black feminist, poststructural, and postcolonial thought, specifically Audre Lorde, Frantz Fanon, Gayatri Spivak, and Michel Foucault, Huckaby investigates the spaces between free speech and silence, action and inaction, life and death, peace and war within the context of threats of wars—international and national—that transform these spaces and the existence within them. Finally, she explores how we prepare ourselves and the world for an existence beyond our destruction, how we make a world less toxic in the potentiality of survival.

In Chapter Three, "'Unbought and Unbossed': On Being Black, Woman, and Transgressive in the Fight for Justice," Valerie Kinloch juxtaposes Black feminisms, biography, autoethnographic events, and historical analysis. Since our research concerns the 2016 presidential election, Kinloch uses biographical content to remind us that Shirley Chisholm was the first Black congresswoman (1968) and first Black person to campaign for the presidency of the United States (1972). Further, Chisholm embodied a particularly important transgressive subjectivity that should be juxtaposed with today's political climate. Kinloch places this history alongside particular feelings of pain and devastation brought on by contemporary events in which Persons of Color have been killed. Chisholm's transgressive subjectivity was marked by her political disposition, ideologies, and commitments to/for humanity (Chisholm, 1973), on the one hand, and by her raced and gendered identities, on the other hand. Kinloch examines how being Black, woman, and transgressive in the fight for public justice (see Fannie Lou Hamer, June Jordan, Audre Lorde, Toni Morrison, Assata Shakur, Alice Walker, etc.) requires us to move toward an "unbought and unbossed" (Melancon, 2014) discourse of/for human rights that center specific situated (and often highly contested) needs for identity politics/identity rights.

In Chapter Four, "Sanity on the Chopping Block, or How to Save Yourself in an Insane World," Yvonna S. Lincoln suggests that action in the public sphere is the only way for researchers to save our sanity in the difficult neoliberal, late capitalist context, especially as it is magnified by the Trump administration in the United States. She advises critical qualitative scholars to expand our public behaviors and think research questions and methodologies differently, in ways that insert the self into national conversations. Acknowledging that personal actions are often viewed as public resistance, she advises scholars to intensify our involvements in everything from taking part in protests to joining conservation, activist, and justice groups. She recognizes that professional lives are often, at best, viewed as private resistance and proposes that these private actions become more public, as well as expanded. Lincoln discusses in some depth a range of actions that include: choosing inquiry that is more comprehensible to a range of audiences (for example, either forgoing the current focus on the "posts" or rethinking the theories/views in ways that are directly applicable to the public as well as more understandable and motivating); conducting work that directly acknowledges the terrain in which we are attempting to survive; and recognizing when we are repeating the past and simply assigning new labels to old ideas and practices. She challenges researchers to always and already tilt toward justice for political resistance as well as knowledge production.

In Chapter Five, "Shuffling the Deck: The 'Woman Card,' Misogyny, and Material-Discursive Complexities of 'Identities' Janet L. Miller employs a complex feminist poststructural analysis to consider varied iterations of misogyny and "the woman card" as both played by and dealt to Hillary. She focuses on interpretations offered by literary as well as academic feminists (Atwood, 2017; Bordo, 2017b; Butler, 2017; Mead, 2017) to further examine, on one hand, contingently situated needs and desires for forms of "identity politics" that enable the fight for and attainment of human rights. On the other hand, the very concepts of misogyny and the "woman card" imply what many critique as essentialized assumptions about any identity category, including biology-related and binary-only versions of woman and man. Assumptions of unitary "identities" seem increasingly inadequate in light of current and proliferating complexities of subjectivities, including those who refuse binary-only assumptions about gender and race, for example. Miller also considers post foundationally oriented research that attends to poststructural theories as both challenged and expanded by perspectives (differently) offered by new materialist, posthuman, and affect theories that dispute reified, singular, and autonomous versions of "identities" of living and nonliving entities, thus potentially opening up possibilities for vitally inclusive versions of "social justice" in education and its broad research arenas. By specifically considering Hillary's defeat in relation to complicatings of unitary implications of misogyny and "the woman card," Miller thus shuffles that deck of cards and all that it represents.

In Chapter Six, "Resisting Patriarchy: Explorations Using a Collaborative Protest Play," Gaile S. Cannella explores a public, collective method to make present the historical scholarship, actions, and struggles of those who have come before. A performance labeled a *protest script* that can be presented using audience participation along with concrete activities and materials is constructed using research on both contemporary news media reports and current critical inquiry that explores misogyny. Direct quotes are used for a large percentage of the play to facilitate the prominence and direct authenticity of a multiplicity of voices. Shorter versions of the play and activities have been used at the end of recent traditional research sessions to remind the participants of past affirmative historical work and many possibilities open to critical scholars.

The final chapter of this volume is a resource guide, designed to give the reader starting points from which to conceptualize research entanglements.

These references represent basic information on critical scholarship, nonviolent forms of resistance and contemporary issues, and websites that cross intersectional boundaries of oppression toward increased justice.

We encourage the reader to use this volume as a starting point for nonviolent justice-oriented research, always/already remembering that justice and equity are "not a Trump issue" (quoted from the online Introduction, Shanks, 2017), even if we use this current circumstance to (re)conceptualize research as illustrated in this volume. As Shanks suggests, we would also hope that researchers would not privilege the current administration by being caught up in "Trump time." Rather, we know that the United States is a country founded in colonial conquest and dominated by racism and misogyny. Further, around the globe, these forms of violence have played out over and over. Perhaps, and hopefully, the dire circumstances imposed by the existence of the current U.S. administration will result in increased action by researchers. However, we will remember that we have been concerned about justice and equity for some time, and necessary actions are ongoing. We should use our current condition to intensify our actions through/with research as well as embolden our efforts, alliances, and collaborative accomplishments.

References

Atwood, M. (2017). What *The Handmaid's Tale* means in the age of Trump. *The New York Times*, March 10. https://www.nytimes.com/2017/03/10/books/review/margaret-atwood-handmaids-tale-age-of-trump.html

Barad, K. (2007). *Meeting the universe halfway: Quantum physics and the entanglement of matter and meaning.* Durham, NC: Duke University Press.

Barthes, R. (2002). The death of the author. In A. McCleary & D. Finkelstein (Eds.), *The book history reader* (pp. 221–224). New York, NY: Routledge.

Bordo, S. (2017a, April 2). The destruction of Hillary Clinton: Sexism, Sanders, and the millennial feminists. *The Guardian*. Retrieved from https://www.theguardian.com/us-news/commentisfree/2017/apr/03/the-destruction-of-hillary-clinton-sexism-sanders-and-the-millennial-feminists

Bordo, S. (2017b). *The destruction of Hillary Clinton.* Brooklyn, NY: Melville House.

Butler, J. (2017, January 18). Reflections on Trump [Online forum post]. https://culanth.org/fieldsights/1032-reflections-on-trump

Cannella, G.S. (2015). Engaging critical qualitative science: Histories and possibilities. In G.S. Cannella, M.S. Perez, & P.A. Pasque (Eds.), *Critical qualitative inquiry: Foundations and futures* (pp. 7–28). Walnut Creek, CA: Left Coast Press.

Cannella, G.S., & Koro-Ljungberg, M. (2017). Neoliberalism in higher education: Can we understand? Can we resist and survive? Can we become without neoliberalism? *Cultural Studies <=> Critical Methodologies, 17*(3), 155–162.

Cannella, G.S., & Lincoln, Y.S. (2011). Ethics, research regulations, and critical social science. In N.K. Denzin & Y.S. Lincoln (Eds.), *The SAGE handbook of qualitative research* (4th ed., pp. 81–90). Thousand Oaks, CA: SAGE.

Cannella, G.S., & Lincoln, Y. (2009). Deploying qualitative methods for critical social purposes. In N.K. Denzin & M.D. Giardina (Eds.), *Qualitative inquiry and social justice* (pp. 53–72). Walnut Creek, CA: Left Coast Press.

Cannella, G.S., & Manuelito, K. (2008). Feminisms from unthought locations: Indigenous worldviews, marginalized feminisms, and revisioning an anticolonial social science. In N.K Denzin, Y.S. Lincoln, & L.T. Smith (Eds.), *Handbook of critical and indigenous methodologies* (pp. 45–59). Thousand Oaks, CA: SAGE.

Chisholm, S. (1973). *The good fight*. New York, NY: HarperCollins.

Cooper, R., & Burrell, G. (1988). Modernism, postmodernism, and organizational analysis: An introduction. *Organizational Studies, 9*(1), 91–112.

Crenshaw, K. (1989). Demarginalizing the intersection of race and sex: Feminist critique of antidiscrimination doctrine, feminist theory, and antiracist politics. *University of Chicago Legal Forum*, Volume 1989, Article 8 https://chicagounbound.uchicago.edu/ucif/vol1989/iss1/8/

Deleuze, G., & Guattari, F. (1987). *A thousand plateaus: Capitalism and schizophrenia*. Minneapolis, MN: University of Minnesota Press.

Denzin, N.K. (1991). *Images of postmodern society*. Newbury Park, CA: SAGE.

Denzin, N.K., & Lincoln, Y.S. (1998). Entering the field of qualitative research. In N.K. Denzin & Y.S. Lincoln (Eds.), *Strategies of qualitative inquiry* (pp. 1–34). Thousand Oaks, CA: SAGE.

Derrida, J. (1978). *Writing and difference*. Alan Bass, trans. London, England: Routledge.

Fine, M. (2018). *Just research in contentious times: Widening the methodological imagination*. New York, NY: Teachers College Press.

Fleck, L. (1979). *Genesis and development of a scientific fact*. Chicago, IL: University of Chicago Press.

Folkers, A. (2016). Daring the truth: Foucault, parrhesia, and the genealogy of critique. *Theory, Culture, and Society, 33*(1), 3–28.

Foucault, M. (2008). *The birth of biopolitics: Lectures at the College de France 1978–1979*. G. Burchell, trans. New York, NY: Palgrave Macmillan.

Foucault, M. (1997). What is critique? In S. Lotringer (Ed.) & L. Hochroth, (Trans.), *The politics of truth*. (pp. 41–81). Los Angeles, CA: Semiotext(e).

Foucault, M. (1977). What is an author? D.F. Bouchard and S. Simon, trans. In D.F. Bouchard (Eds.), *Language, counter-memory, practice* (pp. 113–138). New York, NY: Cornell University Press.

Foucault, M. (1972). *The archaeology of knowledge*. A.M. Sheridan Smith, trans. New York, NY: Palgrave Macmillan.
Glaser, B., & Strauss, A. (1967). *The discovery of grounded theory: Strategies for qualitative research*. Chicago, IL: Aldine.
Guba, E.G. (1990). The alternative paradigm dialog. In E.G. Guba (Ed.), *The paradigm dialog* (pp. 17–27). Newbury Park, CA: SAGE.
Haraway, D. (2015). *Staying with the trouble: Making kin in the Chthulucene*. Durham, NC: Duke University Press.
Haraway, D. (2000). *How like a leaf: An interview with Thyrza Nichols Goodeve*. London, England: Routledge.
hooks, b. (2001). *Salvation: Black people and love*. New York, NY: HarperCollins.
Jackson, Z.I. (2015). Outer worlds: The persistence of race in movement "beyond the human." *GLQ: A Journal of Lesbian and Gay Studies, 21*(2–3), 215–218.
Kincheloe, J., & McLaren, P.L. (1994). Rethinking critical theory and qualitative research. In N.K. Denzin & Y.S. Lincoln (Eds.), *Handbook of qualitative research* (pp. 133–157). Thousand Oaks, CA: SAGE.
King, M.L. (2003). *A testament of hope*. New York: HarperOne. (Original work published 1986)
Koro-Ljungaberg, M. (2016). *Reconceptualizing qualitative research: Methodologies without methodology*. Thousand Oaks, CA: SAGE.
Koro-Ljungberg, M., & Cannella, G.S. (2018). Critical qualitative inquiry: Histories, methodologies, and possibilities. *International Review of Qualitative Research, 10*(4), 327–339.
Latour, B. (2004). Why has critique run out of steam? From matters of fact to matters of concern. *Critical Inquiry, 30*(2), 225–248.
Lerner, G. (1986). *The creation of patriarchy*. New York, NY: Oxford University Press.
Lilla, M. (2016, November 18). The end of identity liberalism. *The New York Times*. https://www.nytimes.com/2016/11/20/opinion/sunday/the-end-of-identity-liberalism.html
Lorde, A. (1984, 2007). *Sister outsider: Essays and speeches*. Berkeley, CA: Crossing Press.
Lincoln, Y.S., & Guba, E.G. (1985). Constructed realities. In *Naturalistic inquiry*, (pp. 70–91). Newbury Park, CA: SAGE.
Lyotard, J.F. (1984). *The postmodern condition: A report on knowledge*. Minneapolis, MN: University of Minnesota Press.
Mead, R. (2017, April 17). Margaret Atwood: The prophet of dystopia. *The New Yorker*. https:www.newyorker.com/magazine/2017/04/17/Margaret-atwood-the-prophet-of-dystopia
Melancon, T. (2014). *Unbought and unbossed: Transgressive Black women, sexuality, and representation*. Philadelphia, PA: Temple University Press.
Moore, J.W. (2016). (Ed.), *Anthropocene or capitalocene?* Oakland, CA: PM Press.

Moore, J.W. (2015). *Capitalism and the web of life: Ecology and the accumulation of capital*. London, England: Verso.

Noys, B. (2011, November). *The discreet charm of Bruno Latour, or the critique of "anti-critique."* Paper presented at the Centre for Critical Theory, University of Nottingham. Retrieved from www.academia.edu/1477950/The_Discret_Charm_of_Bruno_Latour_or_the_critique_of_anti-critique

Popkewitz, T. (1990). Whose future? Whose past? Notes on critical theory and methodology. In E.G. Guba (Ed.), *The paradigm dialog* (pp. 46–66). Newbury Park, CA: SAGE.

Rau, C. (2005, October). *Indigenous metaphors of the heart: Transformative praxis in early childhood education in Aotearoa, privileging Mäori women's educator's voices*. Paper presented at the 13th International Conference on Reconceptualizing Early Childhood Research Theory and Practice, Madison, WI.

Ray, A., & Selinger, E. (2008). Jagannath's Saligram: On Bruno Latour and literary critique after postcoloniality. *Postmodern Culture, 18*(2). Retrieved from http://pmc.iath.virginia.edu/text-only/issue.108/18.2ray_selinger.txt

Seidman, S. (Ed.). (1994). *The postmodern turn*. Cambridge, England: Cambridge University Press.

Shanks, G. (2017). Not a Trump issue—Introduction. *Lateral: Journal of the Cultural Studies Association, 6*(2). Retrieved from https://csalateral.org/issue/6-2/introduction-not-a-trump-issue-shanks/

Steinberg, S. (2012). What's critical about qualitative research? In S. Steinberg & G.S. Cannella (Eds.), *Critical qualitative research reader* (p. ix). New York, NY: Peter Lang.

Strauss, A., & Corbin, J. (1994). Grounded theory methodology: An overview. In N.K. Denzin & Y.S. Lincoln (Eds.), *Handbook of qualitative research* (pp. 273–285). Thousand Oaks, CA: SAGE.

Von, Werlhof, C. (2007). Capitalist patriarchy and the negation of matriarchy: The struggle for a "deep" alternative. In G. Vaughan (Ed.), *Women and the gift economy: A radically different world view is possible* (pp. 139–153). Toronto, Canada: Inanna.

CHAPTER TWO

Difficult Love
Preparations of a Warrior[i]

M. Francyne Huckaby

> *I dreamt I had begun training to change my life, with a teacher who is very shadowy.... I didn't really understand, but I trusted this shadowy teacher. Another young woman who was there told me she was taking a course in "language crazure," the opposite of discrazure (the cracking and wearing away of rock).... It's very exciting to think of me being all the people in this dream.* (Audre Lorde, 1997, p. 13).

LOVE

I WROTE ON November 4th as I sat with my journal at the American Educational Studies Association conference, finding the space I needed for an upcoming session on Transcultural Love and pushing aside my anxieties of the upcoming election. The day before I had performed my monologue, *Walking with Audre Lorde*. I started reading Lorde again a few years ago. I needed help figuring out what to do with dragons, red dragons in particular, what Lorde calls "this capitalist dragon within which we live" (Lorde, 1984/2007, p. 60). The red dragon is greedy, covetous, and obsessed with treasures. It has wings and horns, breathes fire, and is carnivorous, preferring people. With my sister scholars and our performed monologues, *Womanish Ways: Monologues at the Intersections of Race, Gender, and Curriculum Theorizing* (see Baszile, Edwards, & Guillory, 2016), we formed a nurturing and generative space. Eros, the Greek personification of love, was born of chaos and embodied "creative power and harmony" (Lorde, 2007, p. 55). I wanted a kindred space for the next session that would be kin to the erotic, which for Lorde is "an assertion of the life-force of women; of that creative energy empowered, the knowledge and use of which we are now reclaiming"

(p. 55). I wanted to find a space for myself that could resist corruptions and distortions of this source of energy, power, and information.

Love, difficult

I continued writing.

At a family dinner, after I had shared that we needed to prepare for a Trump win, my sister-in-law told us about FiveThirtyEight.com and her habit of checking it. Her offering of this antidote to my paranoia didn't stop me from knowing in my bones and gut that we needed to prepare for shocked and angry people when Trump wins or (and especially) if he loses. I didn't know what it meant to prepare, so I was doing what I could. I collected important documents and cash, bound them in a portable document case, and placed them in a drawer that I could get to quickly. I started adding items to the shopping list—nonperishables, frozen foods, dog food. This is atypical behavior for me. I enjoy the pleasure of surprises in the grocery bags as I put things away or pushing the cart down the aisles and collecting what looks good and tasty. The division of labor my spouse claimed pushed me out of the grocery shopping and laundry duties early in our relationship, so my unexpected encroachment over a line drawn years ago was met with, "How many frozen pizzas do we need? We already have roasted nuts?" I'm used to asking similar questions—but we already have ketchup?—rather than having them turned on me. I surprised myself the weekend before AESA when I answered, "Enough for three months? Three months!" to the question, "How much dog food are you trying to collect?", revealing my subconscious anxiety about the election.

Love, difficult, anger grief

Hope and I are not good friends. If I'm not cautious enough with hope's seductions, the ways it pulls thing out of view (Baudrillard, 1983), I too easily lose myself, forget to practice myself (Foucault, 1997) in the ways I intend, for "[t]he erotic is a measure between the beginnings of our sense of self and the chaos of our strongest feelings" (Lorde, 1984/2007, p. 54). I continued writing my journal entry:

Love, difficult, anger grief — in the sadness I'm struck by this entry. I wrote curving "ness" down into the gravity of my realization. My journal is a space where I jot quick notes, things that I want to remember and work out later. I capture impressions and rarely write full sentences, unless I'm inspired enough to write and don't want to lose the words as I know them at the moment. I'm intentional when

I write prepositions, wanting to signal the location of some importance. I learned to live without prepositions in Papua New Guinea; a dizzying experience at first but quite joyous and freeing once you get used to life without things having to be specific. Returning prepositions to my language upon returning home stressed the imposition and heaviness they have by fixing ideas into locations, onto places. I also avoid articles just because it's easier to get a fleeting idea down by dropping them. So the first part of the entry is quite typical for me. But "*in the* sadness" —it's both a feeling that I had wondered into and a dark place, where I could get stuck. A place I had intentionally, over the previous six months, worked to re-place so that I might be in joy.

When I face difficult times, I remind myself that my elders and ancestors, those who came before dealt with far more, survived through and thrived despite of, that I am made of the same stuff. In "Poetry Is Not a Luxury," Audre Lorde wrote, "For each of us as women, there is a dark place within, where hidden and growing our true spirit rises, 'beautiful/and tough as chestnut/stanchions against (y)our nightmare of weakness/'—and of impotence" (2007, p. 36).

I focus on how I will be, who I will be as my true spirit rises, living potently, in an age of an undisciplined orange regime. This is a battle. Finding that beautiful and chestnut tough place and using it does not have to entail warrior metaphors. But at this junction, I cannot identify a more fitting trope. My battle is not with the people who voted for the now-45th president or those who didn't vote. We are all on this mothership, Earth, together and to give us a chance to live past a few generations, to give some species a chance to live through this century, we cannot—none of us—come out unchanged. My battle is with the systems, ways of thinking, desires, misogyny, bigotry, capitalism, myopic nationalism, neoliberalisms, and the like that make his presidency possible and unaccountable. It's about us and the shifting fractures in our society. We will either find another way or continue to commit mass suicide/murder. That's exactly what I think we are doing through our policies, practices, laws, and interactions that result in death, commit sprit murder (Williams, 1987), and destroy capacity for life and living well. We are at war with ourselves, our very existence, and disguising this fact with political allegiance. I'm drawing my battle lines at the fissures along emotions, truth, and imagination. I want to teach myself a different kind of love.

In the months, weeks, and days before the election, I dreamt heavily, woke frequently—feeling, thinking, writing. I worked to hold onto my dreams, to walk them into the world, to bring them forward into some understanding of their increased interruptions to my sleep. I can easily take my consciousness into my dreams, but these dreams pierced through sleep, rupturing into my waking world. They lingered in my morning rituals, sitting with me over coffee, tugging at me as I fed my puppy, and following me on my walk to campus. I have translated these dreams and their lingerings into poems, to honor Audre Lorde's conception of poetry as "not only dream and vision; it is the skeleton architecture of our lives. It lays the foundations for a future of change, a bridge across our fears of what has never been before" (1984/2007, p. 37).

covered and wrapped
too tight
cant move hard to breathe
my hair pulled straight
bound out of sight

                                            walking to campus
                                       do i, dare i take a right
                          "We do not call 911" above an image of a gun
                       is this what my neighborhood has become

Stripped down
in underwear cold, damp
my kinks crazy, tangled
humidity rules

    At first I dreamt of losses, of becoming more of who I am and yet not myself, of losing the possibilities of who I might, could possibly become. Dangers were a recurrent theme—of avoidance and walking head on into them. But I was silent, always silent, sometimes choosing it and other times forced mute.

i go to speak, moving lips
am i invisible, inaudible
i go to write, my wrist—pain
tell us this, tell us that
i wait, silent

Difficult Love

                                              walking to campus
                                    do i, dare i take a chance
                                                  walk forward
              Trump & Pence, Trump & Pence, Trump & Pence
                                      are they my neighbors
                                                   am i theirs
                                  gallithumpians in residence

refusing to tell
circulation slows, sensations fade
and then a cold blade

The months before the election had already brought heightened hostility, incivility, maybe, quite possibly White fragility (DiAngelo, 2011) or White fatigue (Flynn, 2015). I imagined what I could do as the world becomes more of what it would be and yet not itself, losing possibilities of what it might, could become. I worried about crowd (re)actions to the candidate's words at campaign rallies, their chants, their escalating violence, and promises of legal support by their favored candidate. I witnessed via news shows video footage of crowds turning against attendees and news reporters behind barricades packing up to leave after the candidate labeled them fake news and enemies. Under other circumstances, these images may have seemed more distant, but earlier in 2015, the then-Republican nominee visited Dallas. Reports circulated through the family about the cousin of one of our relatives, a politically engaged young woman. She was a child the last time I saw her in person, but her picture with a group of peers and a potential U.S. president from a previous election cycle adorned a relative's refrigerator for years. At the rally, she was pushed and her scarf pulled off. A citizen, she had every right to attend the rally of a potential candidate for president, whether she supported his candidacy or not. But the crowd read her brown skin and scarf (likely worn for fashion) as reason to make her feel unwelcome. I heard she was not physically hurt but shaken by the experience. As I watched rallies and news feeds that denied the populace what it may need most, forced to imagine what my life might become, what we might become in a nation that returns to such an intense fear of its own because we were made here slave, immigrant, Black and Brown. I suspected this might mean giving up things, walking away, being robbed, having things taken away.

>   forward, I chose
>   past the houses, by trucks
>   speak a hello
>   directly eye-to-eye
>   forcing myself to remain
>   engaged not distant
>   obliging them to speak back
>   notice feelings, just registering them

Refusing silence in my waking world, I wondered what harbinger invaded my dreams. The soundtrack of my dreams was noise, specific yet hard to identify; familiar and chaotic like a favorite spice disguised among unknown flavors. I worked to listen to hear something I could understand. This exercise in lucidity produced, at first, barely noticeable and eventually comfortably audible, my uncle's voice. The sounds could have been any war movie, news reel, or documentary, but shrouded in the affect of a familiar, intergenerational home. Why my uncle? Why his memory? Are my dreams layers of myself piercing through my consciousness? Do my ancestors join me in my dreams (Dillard, 2012)? This momentum, walking out from dreams into interactions brought an understanding. Maybe not *the* correct one, not *the* final one, but one I could work with. Facing impending losses I chose to survive them—at least, and maybe thrive despite them. Now, in the aftermath of the election, I must choose how to do so.

> i hear myself tell my self
> we can live without that, you do without this
> but do not forget; don't you lose it
>
>   choosing
>   as freeing
>   as constraining

Such imaginings were not hard, for I tend to overindulge in the pleasures of pessimism, my antidote to misplaced hope. Giving into (at least in imaginary ways) the potential, possible, probable is necessary to weather shocks and essential for survival. I mourned in these imaginings of being without and shaking off the unnecessary.

Battle Lines

Noticing my language changing, I found myself relinquishing the word *struggle*, as in "being in the struggle," and replacing it with *fight*—"preparing for the fight." I believe or believed myself to be a peace-wielding pessimistic pacifist. I work to avoid violence (that I might encounter as well as that I could inflict). Such a mode of being does not mean being passive or silent, but speaking the truths I have come to know even when risky or dangerous to do so. To live in a just world where powers and vulnerabilities (Gilson, 2011) are not so unequally distributed (Huckaby, 2013), I dare to expect and enact it in my lifetime. Why not? Being a pessimist protects me when humanity disappoints. (If I were an optimist, I might have to turn to a word like *devastate* instead of *disappoint*.) I cannot afford being knocked off my feet in the moments when action is required. Pessimism helps me stay in the struggle, be ready for the fight, and find delight in the spaces where such work is needed less. Fighting is the warrior talk that I began using. I had embraced the poet and scholar Audre Lorde some years prior, but I kept Gamba Adisa—"warrior, she who makes her meaning known" (Lorde, 1980/1997, p. 85) —at a safe distance. I read over these passages more quickly, thought about them less, choosing to focus on her tools, sparks, silence, and whispers. In an entry in her cancer journals, while in St. Croix on April 20, 1986, Lorde wrote:

> As warriors, our job is to actively and consciously survive it for as long as possible, remember that in order to win, the aggressor must conquer, but the resister need only survive. Our battle is to define in ways that are acceptable and nourishing to us, meaning with substance and style. Substance. Our work. Style. True to our selves. (Byrd, Cole, & Guy-Sheftall, 2008, p. 128).

The first battle for this warrior I am (becoming) was not with the 45th president or his supporters, but with myself in this transforming world. Can one be both a pacifist and a warrior? And live into their contradictions? For now, I need to train the warrior I (may) need to be and trust that the pacifist me is already strong enough for a partner.

I don't remember my introduction to war. I've never been *in* war even though my country's been at war my entire life. My uncle returned home safely from the Korean War only to continue to fight daily, relive it continuously. I spent much time as a child in the home he shared with my grandmother and aunt. It was a magical and loving place full of stories, gardening, baking, piano playing, reading, drawing, pickling, crocheting, napping, and warring. My uncle had a deep, booming voice that made his narrations of war vivid. I could see him in dark places, hiding behind landforms and trees, crouching on the ground and in trenches, avoiding shots and bombs; firing weapons himself. Some voices gave orders, some took them and acted. He ran a lot and I could tell when he was avoiding a single bomb or a cascade, rifles from a few people or a mass of soldiers by the sound effects he created. He was a substantial man, well over six feet tall, and when his narrations threw bombs, the sound reverberated through the foundation and walls of the pier-and-beam house. Radio shows should covet his sound effects. By the time I was a teenager, his vocal rememberings fell into the background most days, but sometimes I would sit in the hall outside his door and listen, trying to understand.

When my grandmother or aunt took meals and snacks to his room, he'd command them to leave the tray by the door as if they were his prison guards. His response pained them as they tenaciously cared for him. When I took food, he'd let me bring it to him, often taking a small bite or saying thank you; halting war for a child. Sometimes he smiled, but I suspect those were the times I brought sweets. A few times I took these opportunities to ask questions so I could follow his plot and characters. My questions usually got in the way of his work and he'd dismiss me quickly. So I learned my questions and their answers had to be short. One day he surprised me after I asked about the differences between lieutenants and commanders. He took the opportunity to explain in what seemed like encyclopedic detail the roles and paths to every rank and branch of the U.S. military. I pretended to be a better student than I was, holding an upright pose and facial expression that a soldier might expect from someone who was interested. I now wish I had had the foresight to have taken notes. On occasion he'd look worried in response to my question and say, "I can't talk about that." My family lived through times that I have not and constraints on their freedoms I only know from their stories, reading, and the occasional documentary. I am heir to the same matter and matters that forged them. I am made of the same stuff. I need not worry so much about whether or how to survive.

I am not in war with 45. Even though he is an annoying mosquito buzzing around our heads, I know his bites sting and itch and he knows how to make them fester. We might, some of us or maybe all of us, succumb to diseases passed through his bites that are in the best circumstances uncomfortable and even curable. But in circumstances without treatment, when health is already compromised, they are deadly (e.g., West Nile, chikungunya, malaria). We can rid ourselves of the offending mosquito before or after the bite, but either way does nothing to the pathogens that cause such mosquito-borne diseases. We will continue to face them in variations as we go down the line of succession and vote in future elections. My battle is equally not with the people who voted for this president or even those who did not, or with the electoral college system. Of course I have opinions, perspectives, and insights on each of these that concur and differ from those of other members of this democracy. I am not at war with them, as we are collaborators in the democratic process. We are in this together. My battle is with systems, ways of thinking, and desires. I'm waging war with the shifting fractures in our society, fault lines that reveal just one of the iterations of a global phenomenon of what we might become, could possibly continue on the path of becoming.

Warrior

One cannot be both a warrior and a pacifist; one of us has to stand down, step back, or go—or be made to do so. I have to become honest with myself in realizing that war is about death—drawing a line and fighting to maintain it or die trying. Wars transform, they destroy what was before them, for those who lose as well as those who win. My mother was seven when the Korean War started, and my uncle was a handsome and well-dressed young man. He wore suits tailored to his tall lean body when he came home to visit and had less than a year of college remaining. Grandma lamented, rather frequently, that he was her smartest child. His brilliance seemed to make his postwar condition harder for her. My mother's brother and my grandmother's son did not return home. That part of him was nearly extinguished, replaced by a soldier that could not stop the war. How can I be(come) a warrior without losing myself? How do I quiet the pacifist enough for the warrior to emerge, knowing that this is a transformation that is about death;

suicide/murder to be specific. Might I be a better-skilled warrior if I murdered the pacifist? If the pacifist commits suicide, could that force the warrior to step up? Wouldn't the world be better if people inclined to suicide found ways to live? How do the traumas of suicide and murder corrupt battle, blur the intentions? I know not (fully) which I will do, what I will be(come). I will have to suffice with living in between, facing little and big actions that kill parts of both, a slow suicide-murder transformation. This is life, a slow route to death doing enough to sustain life and not too much to destroy it too quickly. I'm interested in the small episteme(sui)cide (Paraskeva, 2016), the changes that can happen in such close relations, that can transform me into the warrior I need to become, a warrior capable of a different kind of love, one I find most difficult. I'm drawing the battle lines at the fissures along emotion, truth, and imagination.

Even though anxiety and fear were the first emotions to surface as the election approached, I need not battle them as they are useful, can be useful to my awareness of myself and the world. But I need not get lost in them either. For Lorde, "[a]fraid is a country where they issue us passports at birth and hope we never seek citizenship in any other country" (Byrd, et al., 2008, p. 83). I must travel to other places that fear would prevent. Camouflaged as a lack of emotion, numbness is in reality overwhelming and overpowering; it should not be overlooked. Too helpful with survival when not-feeling makes getting through easier, numbness betrays as it lays a trap for merely surviving. Finding ways out of numbness is essential. Anger offers another line of scrimmage. Intensely felt anger that lasts too long and leaves little room for anything else other than revenge and retribution is also a place where one can get lost. I want a different kind of existence. Anger with an attention to the sadness and fear it often accompanies tempers darker desires. Because how people feel has been so important in the rhetoric and discourses that fuel actions, I need an attentiveness to and of emotions—those that I feel and foster as well as those encouraged and sustained through public discourse, media, and politics; finely tuned weapons aimed at battle lines over truth.

I remain unconvinced that we exist in post-truth. The battle of truth, for the rules, over our reasoning, in its shifting, and about its consequences is not new. That the postmodern turn pushed further an opening that pragmatism noticed in truth, from where I sit, is not problematic. Postmodernism continues to offer intellectual tools for making sense of contradictory and complementary truths that coexist, that evolved from divergent mechanisms in the determination of truth. That Foucault (1997) claimed truth is of this world is apropos. Truth is not exempt from the games we play and the battles we fight within its realm. Truth fashioned in one way is upheld when it suits interests and then the very same people can dismiss or invalidate the exact process, structure, reasoning, when the outcome does not work in their favor. When they don't get what they want, they change the rules and shift the criteria for determining truth. Or stated more directly and less poetically—they lie (in a rather complex way). This is not a new dynamic. Marginalized people know this American pastime well; we see it at work, but often find it hard to pull off such plays ourselves primarily because our truths are too often suspect.

Antron McCray, Kevin Richardson, Yusef Salaam, Raymond Santana, and Korey Wise, a group of 14- to 16-year-old teenagers, know truth more difficultly. The situation that took advantage of their proximity to Central Park in New York is an example illustrative of the ways the current White House administration plays games of truth. Natalie Byfield (2014) notes:

> On April 19, we marked the 25th anniversary of the sexual assault of Trisha Meili, the 28-year-old White, female jogger at the center of the 1989 Central Park rape case. I cannot help but ask myself what the ultimate significance of this case will be. The rape along with some assaults and "menacing" acts were used by the media to invent a new form of urban terror labeled "wilding." That a mostly White media used language like "savage," "wolfpack," "animal," and even "feral" to describe the group of African American and Latino teens … accused of rape automatically then, as it does now, points to the racial context in which the media placed Meili's assault.

Easily convicted, they served prison sentences until 2002, when they were exonerated by the confession and DNA match of a serial rapist and murderer. Ads in New York papers taken out by the now-current occupant of the White House were instrumental in drawing attention to the case. National and state changes in subsequent years brought harsher mandatory-minimum sentencing and the subjugation of minors, particularly Black and Latino boys and teenagers, to adult criminal-justice systems.

This president has capitalized on and fueled this transition into post-truth. What is different about this so-called post-truth moment, the very reason it can be labeled as such, is that the acrobatic shifts that recast lies into fact, denials of fact into alternative facts, news into fake news, witnesses into crisis actors, and so forth is the people it affects—people who have not, until now, been on the losing end of games of truth, members of a constituency that thought it wielded the power and influence of truth with agility, expertise, and ease.

If we made a postmodern mistake, I suggest that it was not in exploring truth(s) further. Instead it was forgetting or not understanding that such an endeavor is not exempt from games of truth and plays of power, and that the target of knowledge/power can alter relations of power to create vulnerabilities in positions that seemed more secure. While this moment has much in common with so many others that fell prey to White supremacy, that there is also sustained public opposition (e.g., post-2016 election women's rights marches, support for dreamers, travel ban protests, calling out people who call police, challenging policy that separates children from their parents) signals that truth and how we come to know truth matters.

I wish, so often, that I could be a disinterested, invulnerable party in this political moment. The reality I face with many others is that our futures exist on a knife's edge and I suspect the whole world worries about ending up on the wrong side of the cut—as well as living in a world that makes such a cut—again. In this political climate, some people and groups have ways of making sense of the world that I do not understand, that I have not tried to understand, that I have avoided knowing. A part of me, a vengeful element in my makeup, desires the agency to make such a cut myself. If not for the interventions of my dreams, I could have, would have tried to do so.

I trust the people
when they
are told the truth

                                                 echoed in my head
                                                     Just before dawn
                                                   ripping me from slumber

At first I thought, and still do, that I was remembering a quote from someone or something I read, heard, or saw. I spent weeks trying to track down the quote/idea[ii] through various Internet options, colleagues and friends, books in my collection, as well as films and TV shows I had recently watched. I tried variations on the idea as I could imagine them:

I have faith in the public when it knows the facts.

I believe in humanity when it seeks understanding.

I know not where this idea originated or what sparked its intersection with my waking. Nonetheless, it offered me a new trajectory. No matter how wrong I think a person or group may be in how they come to truth, I have to acknowledge them as thinking beings trying to make sense of a world we share.[iii] The truths we come to know and how we come about them are instrumental in the actions we will take, how games of truth are conducted.

Frontline

Although weapons aim for emotions, the line of scrimmage is truth wielded, claimed, believed. If I am correct in identifying this battle, then the frontline is in the spaces where "truth" is told, tossed, and fired. I believe Trump is a diversion; our real attention needs to turn to the people, our fellow citizens of the world and the people with whom we share this nation. By this, I do not mean that we should ignore or discount the presidency or its current occupant, but to understand how it was made possible and what sustains it. I tried out one tactic to gain a position on the frontline close enough to expand my understandings of the logics of truth at play that differ from logic I know. I live in Texas and am from a family of Texans who were here in the late 1800s. I have always been outside in my home state. I have worked diligently to know myself and foster familial and friend relationships that are affirming. Such intentional actions of self-loving have meant a distancing from other parts of my home. This new tactic required another course of action, for a time.

From the latter part of 2016 through more than half of 2017, I attended regular appointments with a physical therapist. At first I sought to relieve pain and increase range of motion, then to avoid surgery, and finally to recover from surgery. During this time, the therapist moved from a section of a rather large, open-concept facility to a small office space that made it easy for patients to talk with each other. Conversations about politics and sports were abundant, and Trump was frequently discussed. Some years earlier I sought treatment with an allergist who played Fox News in the waiting room. The physician claimed the front desk responded to patient interests. I asked for a different station a few times with little acknowledgment of my request and no change in the channel. Unwilling to support a medical practice that fostered politics antithetical to my own, I switched doctors. I was likewise ready to leave the physical therapist.

Realizing that I had found myself in a safe space shared with Trump supporters who spoke openly in my presence (or a supporter in the presence of agreeable company), I decided to stay and learn. I had so many questions. I figured out which patients were active participants in the political conversations and tried to schedule my appointments to coincide with theirs. I began turning off my critical voice enough to focus on developing my curiosity and willingness to listen. I wanted to seek openings to also be heard. I was not looking for common ground but hoping for openings to encourage reconsiderations. I quickly noticed I did not know how to formulate questions or make comments that would not interrupt, shut down, or support the conversation. For example, I made a comment that I thought was factual and innocuous about one of the early staff members who left the White House. Instead of gaining insights on what people thought about it, my comment fueled a conversation of a "you're fired" ilk. While I was okay with being in the presence of such a conversation in this context, I was not okay with starting it. From then on, I spent most of my time listening and noticing. For the purposes of this chapter, explicating what I experienced in this space may not be important. Furthermore, it was one context, and generalizing about people's ways of thinking and sense-making would likely be more harmful than helpful. What is important is that finding myself outside political isolation, I did not retreat to a more comfortable political space but tried to learn about how people unlike myself understand our shared, although divisive, political world.

I suspect some readers will question why I subjected myself (and now my readers) to this situation, why I risked supporting Trump by staying, and why I am not more focused on discrediting this administration. The simple answer is that life itself, as we know it on this planet, is at stake. By *life* I mean the lives of those of us who will become marginalized and those who will be further marginalized through neglect, steady violations, and outright violence. I also mean further destruction of the planet capable of sustaining and renewing life, which we may push to its limits in ways that jeopardize lives and life. I find the science that shows us the ways our actions as humans are destroying the capacity for life as we know it trustworthy. We may be past the tipping point. But I am not giving up on a physical world—this spaceship of ours, Mother Earth. The remnants, toxins, and poisons of our existence may threaten future potential life before it has a chance, millennia, if not eons, from now. I need ways, we need ways to engage and communicate in ways that reach beyond separate political realms, ways to make sense to people inclined to discount our warnings. Along with these actions I also vote, protest, and offer support, resist, and stay informed. Learning in the spaces of the frontlines (well, those spaces that I can access) of this truth battle is an addition I think worthy of some time, because communication within our politico-epistemological camps and using these same communication strategies across camps may do the opposite of what we intend.

I've already confessed to my pessimistic tendencies. I can imagine a different kind of world, spend much of my life working for it, and still not expect to see it, all the while anticipating and waiting for horrendous things to happen. The series of the last three presidential elections has taught me that the (un)imaginable is possible. While I wished somewhere deep inside and unspoken, I did not believe a Black president would be elected in my lifetime or survive a term in office without an assassination attempt, let alone two terms; nor did I expect a woman to receive a popular vote majority of nearly three million. I wanted these things but did not believe the nation ready. In 2015 a Trump candidate was unimaginable to me, and within a year I feared his presidency was likely. The (un)imaginable is possible. One important battle line, one I must endeavor to win, is with my own disbelief, as subtle as it may be at times. It halts and even sabotages possibilities. Needed is a politics that can wildly imagine and believe liberatory forms of justice and love into being, even into the spaces where retribution and vengeance may seem more deserving. This is a difficult love.

References

Baszile, D. T., Edwards, K. T., & Guillory, N. A. (2016). *Race, gender, and curriculum theorizing: Working in womanish ways (Race and education in the twenty-first century)*. Lanham, MD: Lexington Books.

Baudrillard, J. (1983). *Simulations*. P. Foss, P. Patton, & P. Beitchman, trans. New York, NY: Simiotext(e).

Byfield, N. (2014, May 27). The legacy of the Central Park jogger "wilding" case. *Huffpost*. Retrieved from https://www.huffingtonpost.com/natalie-byfield/the-legacy-of-the-central_b_5398013.html

Byrd, R. P., Cole, J. B., & Guy-Sheftall, B. (Eds.). (2008). *I am your sister: Collected and unpublished writings of Audre Lorde*. New York, NY: Oxford University Press.

DiAngelo, R. (2011). White fragility. *International Journal of Critical Pedagogy, 3*, 54–70.

Dillard, C. B. (2012). *Learning to (re)member the things we've learned to forget: Endarkened feminisms, spirituality, & the sacred nature of research & teaching*. New York, NY: Peter Lang.

Flynn, J. (2015). White fatigue: Naming the challenge in moving from an individual to a systemic understanding of racism. *Multicultural Perspectives, 17*(3), 115–124.

Foucault, M. (1997). The ethics of the concern for self as practice of freedom. In P. Rabinow (Ed.), *Michel Foucault: Ethics: subjectivity and truth* (vol. 1). New York, NY: New Press.

Gilson, E. (2011). Vulnerability, ignorance, and oppression. *Hypatia, 26*, 308–332.

Huckaby, M. F. (2013). Much more than power: The pedagogy of promiscuous Black feminism. *International Journal of Qualitative Studies in Education, 26*(5), 567–579.

Lorde, A. (1997). *The cancer journals*. San Francisco, CA: Aunt Lute Books. (Original work published 1980)

Lorde, A. (2007). *Sister outsider: Essays and speeches*. Berkeley, CA: Crossing Press. (Original work published 1984)

Paraskeva, J. M. (2016). *Curriculum epistemicide: Towards an itinerant curriculum theory*. New York, NY: Routledge.

Williams, P. (1987). Spirit-murdering the messenger: The discourse of fingerprinting as the law's response to racism. *Miami Law Review, 42*, 127–157.

Endnotes

i Parts of the paper are inspired by the play *White Rabbit, Red Rabbit* by Nassim Soleimanpour (2010). If it were any other kind of play, I would reference it explicitly. No one is supposed to know anything about the play before seeing it except the title, the actor receives the script on stage and can only perform the play once, and the contents of the play must be kept secret. The author wrote the play as an experiment while in Iran and not free to travel because he refused war. This chapter is not about the play, but sections of my work here and my warrior journey in the realm of rabbits have more clarity because of the play.

ii If you have a reference for this concept, please do share with me.

iii Some may just want to oppress and kill, and we need ways to make their powers impotent. But I will brake this realization for now.

CHAPTER THREE

"Unbought and Unbossed"
On Being Black, Woman, and Transgressive in the Fight for Justice

Valerie Kinloch

SHIRLEY ANITA ST. Hill Chisholm was born on November 30, 1924. During her lifetime, she was an educator, an early education consultant, a human rights activist, a social reformer and political strategist, and a staunch supporter for educational equity and racial and gender equality. In fact, Chisholm was one of the founding members of the Congressional Black Caucus (1969), and she became the first Black Congresswoman (1968) and the first Black person to campaign with a major political party for the presidency of the United States (1972). She embodied a particularly important transgressive subjectivity that should be examined in relation to today's political climate. It is a transgressive subjectivity that recognizes, to use her words, that "women are a majority of the population, but they are treated like a minority group [because] the prejudice against them is so widespread ..." (Chisholm, 1970a, p. 20). It is the embodiment and the sheer essence of this transgressive subjectivity that allowed her to acknowledge, write about, and exist with what she believed society, writ large, viewed as her "two handicaps" (p. 20)—being a woman and being Black. In her book *Unbought and Unbossed,* Chisholm (1970a) asserts, "I was the first American citizen to be elected to Congress in spite of the double drawbacks of being female and having skin darkened by melanin" (p. 19).

In other words, Chisholm's transgressive subjectivity, I contend, was visibly marked by her political disposition, ideologies, and commitments to and for humanity, on the one hand, and by her raced and gendered identities (of Woman-ness and Blackness), on the other hand. Her transgressive subjectivity can be situated within what Melancon (2014) references as "an almost exclusively white and male-dominated political terrain" (p. 1). It was both a political terrain and an electoral arena that afforded little to no seats to women and People of Color, and that upheld, and continues to uphold, a status quo steeped in misogyny, violence, erasure, and in what bell hooks (2001) calls "white supremacist capitalist patriarchy" (p. 72). Yet Chisholm remained relentless in her pursuit of equality, knowing the urgency of "breaking with tradition" in order to confront the "sanctions that society will immediately impose upon us" (PageWise, 2002). In "breaking with tradition," she intentionally fought for the rights of children, women, and People of Color disenfranchised by and within an oppressive economic, educational, and political system.

Chisholm's relentlessness and, hence, her transgressive subjectivity, were visible in her decision to run for U.S. president "in spite of hopeless odds...to demonstrate the sheer will and refusal to accept the status quo" (Chisholm, 1970a, p. xv). Boldly, she insisted that "the next time a woman runs, or a black, or a Jew or anyone from a group that the country is 'not ready' to elect to its highest office, I believe that he or she will be taken seriously." (Chisholm, 1973, p. 3). She also insisted: "I ran because somebody had to do it first. In this country, everybody is supposed to be able to run for President, but that has never really been true" (Chisholm, 1973, n.p.). Chisholm's relentlessness and transgressive subjectivity are, indeed, indicative of an inherent refusal to be encumbered, to be contained, to embody an apologetic form of resistance to injustice, and to operate within racial as well as masculinist, or gendered, domination. These things have long (mis) characterized the role of women, especially Black women, in relations involving politics, policies, and power. She believed and lived her life knowing that "women in this country must become revolutionaries" and "must refuse to accept the old, the traditional roles and stereotypes" (Chisholm, 1970a, pp. xvi–xvii).

Considering the never-ending confrontations with "white supremacist capitalist patriarchy" (hooks, 2001, p. 72) experienced by Chisholm and endured by other women still today, I discuss how being Black, woman, and transgressive in the fight for justice requires us to move toward an "unbought and unbossed" discourse or identity politics. This is a discourse that is both of and for human rights and that centers the specific, situated, and often highly contested need for identity politics and identity rights. Additionally, this "unbought and unbossed" politics is unquestionably steeped in antiracist, antihomophobic, and antixenophobic epistemological and ideological understandings of justice, equity, and the rights of all human beings. In my case, I place an explicit focus on what an "unbought and unbossed" discourse means for Black people who have experienced and have emerged from larger histories of systemic violence, marginalization, and other oppressions. For example, in addition to Shirley Chisholm, the lives, leadership, and legacies of Black women, including rights activist Fannie Lou Hamer, poet-activist June Jordan, writer-womanist-activist Audre Lorde, writer-educator Toni Morrison, and liberationist-activist Assata Shakur, among many others, solidify for me the never-ending significance of embodying a discourse and disposition that is "unbought and unbossed."

The aforementioned Black women motivate me to continually consider larger questions about the important role of transgressive subjectivities in theory, praxis, and politics; the specific research methodologies and pedagogies that support transgressive subjectivities through orientations that are humanizing and justice specific; and the ways in which being relentless and transgressive, particularly in the spirit of Shirley Chisholm, can produce tangible solutions for freedom and for surviving our current political reality of hatred, violence, racism, and homophobia. I take inspiration from the work and ways of being of Black women who have been, and remain, relentless in their individual and collective pursuit of justice. Thus, in this brief essay, I offer what I see as a necessary stance toward being "unbought and unbossed" in the push to *transgressively* embody a justice, equity, and rights stance. Doing these things from my own positionality as Black, as Woman, and as Transgressive in the fight for justice requires that I first acknowledge devastations, especially regarding the killing of Black girls and women in this country, that motivate this work. Then, I talk about devastations and dominant epistemologies, resistances, and then the reactions of three Black women to the 2016 U.S. presidential election.

"Unbought and Unbossed": Devastations

As I contemplate what it means to be "unbought and unbossed" (Chisholm, 1970a, 1973), particularly in relation to being Black, Woman, and Transgressive, I am aware that the fight for justice is never-ending. This is the case, given that the fight is rooted within an oppressively and explicitly racist, classist, and sexist historical context that also defines the current sociopolitical moment in which we find ourselves. It is a moment, for instance, in which a discourse of hate, intolerance, and dehumanization seems to dominate and devastate every fabric of our human lives. To make this argument, one need only look to some of the increased public displays of hatred within our very own country, including the government-initiated separation of children from families, the state-sanctioned killings of Black and Brown people, the ICE raids and arrests, and, among many others, the plethora of racism and violence occurring on college campuses. Additionally, it is also a moment that has encouraged many of us to act and agitate more bravely for the rights of People of Color, Communities of Color, and LGBTQIA+ communities, and for the rights of our children, whose lives are constantly under assault. This necessary acting and agitating for freedom, justice, and humanity has defined the importance of such efforts as today's Black Lives Matter Movement, the West Virginia Teachers' Strike, #EqualPay for Women, #NoDAPL, and, among other needed and significant movements, #FlintWaterCrisis.

Thus, in my contemplations of being "unbought and unbossed," I first name and acknowledge some very painful devastations, on a continually growing list of many others, that move me toward or, to say it more directly, ground me in, an "unbought and unbossed" identity politics. This politics is situated within "the Fighting Shirley Chisholm—Unbought and Unbossed" stance of engaging in meaningful, sociopolitically conscious action (for freedom and liberation) that can positively impact the world. And doing so with a "bold posture and obvious willingness to fail" (Chisholm, 1970a, p. 191). One way to do this is by following Chisholm's (1970a) advice: to "act out on ... principles" by being a "catalyst for change" (p. 197). Thus, I have chosen to begin in a place of devastations as I seek, myself, to catalyze change as Black, as Woman, and as Transgressive wanting justice.

Devastations: For me, the murders of Black girls and women will always be devastating. The 2013 murder of Miriam Carey, for example, is devastating. She was killed by U.S. Secret Service and Capitol Police officers in Washington, D.C. Carey, a 34-year-old Black woman who worked as a dental hygienist in Stamford, Connecticut, was said to have driven her car into a checkpoint near the White House, and as she attempted to make a U-turn, she hit "an officer who was trying to move a barricade into her path, before driving away, according to an affidavit filed in support of a search warrant" (Almasy, 2014). Although there were conflicting news accounts, one thing remains certain: Carey was struck and killed by gunfire while her 1-year-old child, who was not physically harmed, was in the back seat of the car.

Devastations: I remain devastated by the 2015 murder of Sandra Bland, a Black woman who was stopped for a minor traffic violation (she did not signal a lane change) not too far from the campus of Prairie View A&M University. Three days after the traffic stop and arrest, Bland was found dead in a jail cell in Waller County, Texas. Countless people across the nation have marched in protest of her death and, as a result, Waller County was heavily scrutinized for this controversial arrest and subsequent suspicious death. Bland became an icon of the Black Lives Matter movement. She lives on in the freedom work of many people across the country.

Similar to how I feel about the killing of Sandra Bland, I also continue to be devastated by the 2016 murder of Tanisha Anderson, a Black woman who was experiencing a mental health episode outside her home before being killed by police officers in Cleveland, Ohio. News account after news account, the story remains the same: "Tanisha Anderson's family can't help but think about her every time they walk down the street outside her house, because that's where police restrained her shortly before she died, not far from the tall tree in the front yard" (Dean, 2015). The killing of Anderson, under any circumstances, is devastating, to say the least.

Devastations: The public assaults and attacks on Black children will always be painfully devastating. Take, for example, the year 2015, when teenagers in bathing suits were victimized as a White police officer pointed a gun at them and then shoved a young Black girl's face into the ground while placing a knee in her back. This was done in an effort to "subdue" her, all the while as the officer used vulgar language toward the gathered teenagers. This happened in McKinney, Texas, and was caught on videotape by a White teenager, who stated, "You can see in part of the video where he [the officer] tells us to sit down, and he kinda like skips over me and tells all my African-American friends to go sit down." (Capehart, 2015).

Devastations: Violence and acts of hatred, regardless of where they happen, are always terribly devastating, and the devastation increases, at least for me, when they surface inside schools. In 2015, in Columbia, South Carolina, a Black girl, sitting at a desk inside a classroom with her peers, was assaulted by a White resource officer and former sheriff's deputy. The officer grabbed the student by the neck, flipped her backward out of her desk, and dragged and threw her across the floor. Instead of being protected, nurtured, and cultivated by adults within the context of schools, Black children are often viewed and treated as adults. In fact, the report "Girlhood Interrupted: The Erasure of Black Girls' Childhood," found that "adults think that black girls are less innocent, less in need of protection and nurturing, and seem older than similarly aged white girls, which could lead to stiffer penalties in school" (Associated Press, 2017). Just devastating!

Devastations: Another violating devastation is not being protected and safeguarded in our own communities and homes by those who dedicate their lives to protecting us. In 2017, Charleena Lyles, a Black woman in Seattle, Washington, was killed inside her apartment after she called the police to report a burglary. Lyles, who had a documented history of mental health concerns, was pregnant at the time. Three of her children (ages 1, 4, and 11) were home at the time of their mother's murder. This murder is devastating for all of us, and I would assume that it is especially devastating for Lyles's children.

There is no way to escape the pain of these devastations. In fact, they exemplify levels of hatred that get enacted onto people, especially Black people and other People of Color, in the United States. The devastations that I have briefly described are just some on a longer list, a list that also includes the lives of women, men, and Children of Color such as Rekia Boyd, Michael Brown, William Chapman, Jamar Clark, and Alberta Spruill. The list also includes the names of Shelley Frey, Kayla Moore, John Crawford III, Terence Crutcher, Samuel DuBose, Ezell Ford, and Eric Garner. We cannot forget that this same list includes the names of Kyam Livingston, Freddie Gray, Kimani Gray, Akai Gurly, Dontre Hamilton, and Eric Harris. This list also includes the lost lives of Michelle Cusseaux, Anthony Hill, Meagan Hockaday, Corey Jones, Charley Leundeu Keunang, and Renisha McBride. Among so many other Black and Brown lives that have been violently taken from us, this list also includes Jeremy McDole, Laquan McDonald, Antonio Martin, Trayvon Benjamin Martin, Jerame Reid, Tamir Rice, Tony Robinson, Jonathan Sanders, Walter Scott, and, among so many others, the Charleston Nine.

As a way to process these devastations, I turn to Shirley Chisholm (1970a), who writes: "From the beginning I felt that there were only two ways to create change for black people in this country—either politically or by open armed revolution. Malcolm defined it succinctly—the ballot or the bullet." She continues: "Since I believe that human life is uniquely valuable and important, for me the choice has to be the creative use of the ballot. I still believe I was right. I hope America never succeeds in changing my mind" (p. 164).

Devastations and Dominant Epistemologies

Daily, I think about what it means to be Black, Woman, and Transgressive. This is the case, given that I am Black, a Woman, and a Transgressive, breathing, living, and always becoming with other Black Women Transgressives in a society that continually disavows and disregards our intellectualism, activism, feminisms, and humanity. There is no question that the lives of Black people, and especially of Black girls and women across the entire globe, have been devalued and remain undervalued in public discourses about education, freedom, humanity, justice, and even politics. In fact, as Patricia Hill Collins (2000) writes in *Black Feminist Thought: Knowledge, Consciousness, and the Politics of Empowerment*:

> The shadow obscuring this complex Black women's intellectual tradition is neither accidental nor benign. Suppressing the knowledge produced by any oppressed group makes it easier for dominant groups to rule because the seeming absence of dissent suggests that subordinate groups willingly collaborate in their own victimization. Maintaining the victimization of Black women and our ideas not only in the United States, but in Africa, the Caribbean, South America, Europe and other places where Black women now live, has been critical in maintaining social inequalities. (p. 3)

Patricia Hill Collins's point is clear—that is, dominant epistemologies and power structures operate throughout society in ways that seek to perpetually deny, or subordinate, Black women's credibility, theoretical traditions, feminist intellectual productions, and political power. In so doing, "social inequalities" are maintained (Collins, 2000, p. 3). Yet this attempt at making the lives of Black girls and women invisible have not discouraged Black Women Transgressives from engaging in "intellectual work, and to have our ideas matter" (Collins, 2000, p. 3). In addition to "Ama Ata Aidoo, Buchi Emecheta, and Ellen Kuzwayo who have used their voices to raise important issues that affect Black African women,"

Collins (2000) also recognizes that "Sojourner Truth, Anna Julia Cooper, Ida B. Wells-Barnett, Mary McLeod Bethune, Toni Morrison, Barbara Smith, and countless others have consistently struggled to make themselves heard" (p. 3). In my opinion, these women represent Black Women Transgressives committed to making more visible the lives, activism, and intellectualism of Black girls and women. They are, to use Chisholm's phrase, "unbought and unbossed."

These Black Women Transgressives have pushed against dominant epistemologies and power structures that operate in ways that harm Black women's bodies and endanger Black women's survival. In *pushing against,* they have operated within a dialectical relationship "of oppression and activism, then tension between the suppression of African-American women's ideas and our intellectual activism in the face of that suppression," and according to Collins (2000), this "constitutes the politics of U.S. Black feminist thought" (p. 3). Insofar as naming the devastations I described earlier and challenging dominant epistemologies that would have us ignore those devastations, Collins (2000) reminds us that "understanding this dialectical relationship is critical in assessing how U.S. Black feminist thought—its core themes, epistemological significance, and connections to domestic and transnational Black feminist practice—is fundamentally embedded in a political context that has challenged its very right to exist" (pp. 3–4).

This latter point is especially important to note because dominant epistemologies and power structures get enacted in ways that expect Black women to save the world from the world itself. This saving, I argue, includes the false expectation that Black women will save the world from patriarchy and capitalism only when these things begin to infringe on the rights of White people. Take, for instance, the 2016 presidential election, when Black women showed up and showed out. We turned out to support Hillary Clinton to become the U.S. president by an overwhelming 94%, in comparison to the outrageously low 53% of White women who voted for Clinton. This is an indication of how dominant epistemologies invite Black women to *side with them* and to *embrace their ways of being,* only to ridicule and dehumanize us while fooling us to not love and save ourselves.

Hence, my devastations. My devastations with those who believe that Hillary Rodham Clinton was the first woman to campaign with a major political party for the presidency of the United States (Shirley Chisholm did not get the Democratic nomination, but she fought hard). My devastations with the murders of Black girls and women in this country that go unpunished. My devastations with the reality that being Black, a Woman, and Transgressive are already marked within a dichotomous, faulty, and to say it more clearly, dangerous relationship. It is a relationship that falsely constructs Black women as *needing* help while also *being* the help. This duality—of being falsely positioned as simultaneously needing and being—materializes for Black girls and women every day within this very patriarchal, capitalist society.

Resisting Needing and Being the Help

I have arrived at this very moment and in conversation with the authors of this book who are thinking about "Surviving and Countering Patriarchal Whitelash: Public Education and Resistance Research by 'Nasty Women'?"— the focus of our panel presentation at the 2018 American Educational Research Association annual meeting. We have shared concerns with, as Yvonna S. Lincoln and Gaile S. Cannella name it, "employing critical qualitative inquiry to mount nonviolent resistance." Yet, I recognize that my individual concern is explicitly connected to a type of violence that continues to get enacted onto Black and Brown people in this nation. Thus, I have no choice but to recognize the murders of Black people, and especially Black girls and women. I must recognize the confluence of racism and capitalism, which points to the power of patriarchy and the undermining of human and civil rights. From educational, economic, and religious rights, to migration rights, women and girls' rights, Black peoples' rights, and trans rights, the confluence is both powerful for some and lethal for others. I also recognize, as does scholar Leigh Patel (2017), "that systems of oppression operate simultaneously but also that they cannot breathe without each other." For example, according to Patel, "ableism begets racism [and] racism quickens with capitalism and heteropatriarchy."

In terms of what happened, politically, in 2016: I am not surprised that Hillary Rodham Clinton lost her bid for the presidency to #45. I was not surprised then and, admittedly, I am still not surprised today, particularly because this type of loss has never not been anticipated by Black women in this country— that is, the explicit workings and intersections of misogyny, capitalism, systemic violence, racism, and other forms of state- and nation-sanctioned oppressions have always been a part of the fabric of Black life in the United States. These things have always assaulted Black people, Black communities, Black love, and Black women's humanity. In fact, these things have always existed and operated against us. I know that this is not new—that the most qualified person lost to a racist, given that colonization has never been, and will never be just a "bad" friend that Black women can "just" accept. For we have always known, as author and social critic James Baldwin (1970) wrote in a powerful "Open Letter" to activist Angela Yvonne Davis, "If they come for you in the morning, they will be coming for us that night" (p. 18).

Additionally, Black women have never not had to confront the reality of "white supremacist capitalist patriarchy," to use hooks's (2001) words, and most times, alone, by ourselves, with only the unwavering love of other Black women. We have never not had to deal with questions of "what to do next?" We have always had to live against what many now see, today, as patriarchal, capitalist whitelash against our daily lives and ways of being in this world. In fact, we have never not had to stare violence and hatred in the face as we have embodied the will and courage to always stand on the front lines to protest the systemic oppression waged against the Black body. And, so, Hillary's loss of the 2016 presidential election was unfortunate, but not surprising.

Maybe it was not surprising because many of us know that the structure of patriarchy is powerful and deadly when it is being threatened by change—especially in the presence of multiple race and gender identities. I was not surprised by what happened in 2016, a year and a time that some of us assumed Hillary was the first woman to campaign with a major political party in pursuit of the U.S. presidency. While one could argue that Hillary Clinton embodied a particularly important transgressive subjectivity in her bid for the presidency, one could also contend that her transgressive subjectivity should have been more firmly grounded in Chisholm's Black woman's transgressive subjectivity of being "unbought and unbossed," which parallels the larger struggle for Black women's rights. Or, maybe not. What I do know is that the day after the 2016 presidential elections was a day of unsurprised shock for me and for other Black women. Let me offer an example of this unsurprising shock and move toward being unbought and unbossed.

Being "Unbought and Unbossed": An Occasion

We sat in our university office inside Arps Hall, Room 153, and we just shook our heads. I wore all black—black pants, a black top, and black shoes the day after 45 was announced the incoming president of the United States. It was the day after we were told what many thought (and what we hoped, but questioned) to be true: that Hillary Rodham Clinton was going to be our next president. But that was actually a lie. I admitted to Ryann and Halima and then, eventually, to Nicole, Tanja, and Carlotta—Black women who worked with me in the Office of Diversity, Inclusion, and Community Engagement in the College of Education and Human Ecology at Ohio State University—that I was not unbothered. I was, but it was a different kind of not being unbothered from the one I experienced in 2012 when President Barack Obama and Joe Biden were facing off with Mitt Romney and Paul Ryan. In November 2012, I had regular headaches and constant ear ringing. I could not fully sleep at night, and the day after the 2012 election, these discomforts all went away. Barack Obama was reelected, and for many reasons (some that might be conflicting) I felt that I could rest slightly with this victory. In some ways, I assumed the same thing (a Democratic win) was going to happen in 2016, but that proved wrong. And I remain unsurprised.

The day after the 2016 election, Halima walked into the office and said, "There's no reason for Black people to vote in U.S. elections anymore." Ryann stared at her. Halima said, "But for real, why are we voting when racists always win anyway? All the time." Ryann just stared at her. Halima continued, "I'm just tired of all this. I am! And what's the benefit to us? That's why I'm thinking that it's pointless to vote anyway." Ryann looked at me and I said, "Because our ancestors died fighting for us to have the right to vote. Because for change to happen, we must continue to seek change, engage in it, knowing that we are always working against and in the face of misogyny, capitalism, systemic violence, racism, and state- and nation-sanctioned oppressions."

Ryann said, "Righhhttttt. Exactly!" And then Halima added, "You right. But the racists always win. Even when there's a white woman in the mix. Even the white woman can't win." Ryann said, "Righhhttttt. Exactly. That's true, but they win more often than we [Black women] win. But ..." And the "but" is what we all already knew ... *but* that even when a White man who spews racist, sexist, and classist beliefs runs against a White woman... even he still wins. *But* that's because of the racial and gendered nature of patriarchy (White and men). *But*...

Halima starred at the floor and said, "Black people always gotta suffer because of what other people do," to which Ryann asserted, "well, or not do, and even still, we have to still vote." What I wished I had said in that moment was what James Baldwin (1970) wrote to Angela Yvonne Davis, that "We must fight for your life as though it were our own—which it is—and render impassable with our bodies the corridor to the gas chamber" for, if "we know, and do nothing, we are worse than the murderers hired in our name" (p. 18).

But I wish I had said to Halima that Hillary Rodham Clinton's loss and 45's win represent moments situated in an ongoing, dangerous, tiring battle for liberty and justice within a majority-operated White society in which many Black people daily encounter violence, racism, and social inequalities because, as Baldwin (1962) tells us, some White people are "still trapped in a history which they do not understand" (pp. 8–9).

But I wish I had pointed her to Baldwin's (1962) essay, "My Dungeon Shook: Letter to My Nephew on the One Hundredth Anniversary of the Emancipation," in which he writes about a history that has allowed White people to believe in Black inferiority and White superiority, even when "many of them, indeed, know better" (p. 9). Yet as Baldwin explains, "people find it very difficult to act on what they know. To act is to be committed, and to be committed is to be in danger. In this case, the danger, in the minds of most white Americans, is the loss of identity" (p. 9). Hence, the loss of the presidency to the last remaining person we chose to believe in... Hillary.

But I didn't. I did not point Halima or Ryann or myself to these responses or to Baldwin's counsel. We sat there—Halima, Ryann, and me—with broken hearts at what White America had done to us, yet again. Our brokenness was more about how patriarchy and racism, even when visibly present and staring at everyone—continue to dominate in harmful ways that negatively impact our whole being. *But* even in our feelings of hopelessness and powerlessness, we are guided by "the Fighting Shirley Chisholm—Unbought and Unbossed" stance. What we did say to each other was that we will continue to stand, knowing that we are from Black women's lives, struggles, intellectual traditions, and histories of abuse and commitment. And, so, Hillary lost. She lost! *But* she did not lose as much as Black women have lost in the history of this country. And we continue fighting for justice, equity, and the rights of Black people in ways that are, and will forever be, "unbought and unbossed."

Some Last Words

But this is not a conclusion; it is a continuation. It is a reminder, if we need one, that Black women have always been revolutionaries and have always been committed to pursuing equality. The 2016 election is a painful reminder of the work that we must continue to do in relation to each other. In doing this work which, to use Chisholm's words, represents a "breaking with tradition," we must be clear that "we must prepare ourselves educationally, economically, and psychologically in order that we will be able to accept and bear with the sanctions that society will immediately impose upon us" (Chisholm, 1970b, p. 4). *But* this has always been and remains a large part of the work of Black Women Transgressives who know that we are "unbought and unbossed."

References

Almasy, S. (2014). Woman killed during D.C. chase was shot five times from behind, autopsy. CNN. Retrieved from https://www.cnn.com/2014/04/08/us/miriam-carey-autopsy/index.html

Associated Press. (2017). The "adultification" of Black girls: Less protection, more discipline. NBC News. Retrieved from https://www.nbcnews.com/news/nbcblk/adultification-black-girls-less-protection-more-discipline-n777591.

Baldwin, J. (1970). An open letter to my sister, Angela Y. Davis. In A. Davis (Ed.), *If they come in the morning: Voices of resistance* (pp. 11–19). New York, NY: Third World Press.

Baldwin, J. (1962). *The fire next time*. New York, NY: Vintage International.

Capehart, J. (2015). The McKinney, Texas pool party: More proof that "black children don't get to be children." *Washington Post*. Retrieved from https://www.washingtonpost.com/blogs/post-partisan/wp/2015/06/10/the-mckinney-texas-pool-party-more-proof-that-black-children-dont-get-to-be-children/?utm_term=.7a8b2d9e2d3e

Chisholm, S. (1973). *The good fight*. New York, NY: HarperCollins.

Chisholm, S. (1970a). *Unbought and unbossed*. Boston, MA: Houghton Mifflin.

Chisholm, S. (1970b). Racism and anti-feminism. *The Black Scholar*, 1(3–4), 40–45.

Collins, P.H. (2000). *Black feminist thought: Knowledge, consciousness, and the politics of empowerment* (2nd ed.). New York, NY: Routledge.

Dean, M. (2015). "Black woman unnamed": How Tanisha Anderson's bad day turned into her last. *Guardian*. Retrieved from https://www.theguardian.com/us-news/2015/jun/05/black-women-police-killing-tanisha-anderson.

hooks, b. (2001). *Salvation: Black people and love*. New York, NY: HarperCollins.

Melancon, T. (2014). *Unbought and unbossed: Transgressive Black women, sexuality, and representation.* Philadelphia, PA: Temple University Press.

PageWise. (2002). Shirley Chisholm biography. Retrieved from http://archive.is/14Y8t

Patel, L. (2017). Rejecting a politics of inclusion. [Blog post.] https://decolonizing.wordpress.com/2017/07/27/rejecting-a-politics-of-inclusion/.

CHAPTER FOUR

Sanity on the Chopping Block
Or How to Save Yourself in an Insane World

Yvonna S. Lincoln

THERE ARE TEXTS and subtexts, threads to collusion and subthreads to hacking. Among the threads that receive little press is the uptick in the number of people—one would presume liberals ("libtards") and progressives, likely Democrats—seeking psychiatric and psychological help. If I had any brains, I would be one of them. Instead, I text/rail at my sister night after night, usually beginning with "I am losing my mind."

It is a sign of serious toxicity in the body politic when thousands of new patients are seeking psychological help to deal with what appears to be a criminal national administration, supported by a corrupt party that refuses to acknowledge that there is something going on which is frighteningly not "normal." Campuses are not immune to the hot and sometimes violent culture wars going on within society; indeed, the First Amendment is being fought out on the front pages of newspapers, in the media, and in the *Chronicle of Higher Education*.

Consequently, some of the individuals seeking help in understanding, or believing, or comprehending what is going on in Washington are likely professors. Indeed, the Secretary of Education appears to be cooperating with the erosion or outright destruction of Obama-era regulations, particularly regarding mounting student debt among recent higher education graduates. And those among us deeply involved with K–12 public education are rightly alarmed by the push to extend private schools, charter schools, and vouchers at the expense of the public schools. As well, massive proposed cuts to the budgets for the National Science Foundation and educational research more broadly signal not only a constricted diet of research funding, but also this administration's general disregard for research and science of all kinds.

It is no wonder educational professionals are alarmed, depressed, shocked, horrified, saddened, fearful, despairing, furious, and appalled. How do we teach in this environment? How do we conduct research? For whom do we conduct research, when it is clear the policy community is set to ignore us? How do we support our research? Educate and support graduate students? Prepare teachers?

It would appear the faculty has a serious reexamination to undergo, and sooner rather than later. One possibility is a rethinking of the curriculum (in all kinds and levels of institutions), so that students are given a much stronger preparation in how to support a democracy and how to deal with the growing pluralism that has given rise to so much resentment. Colleges and universities are often accused of being bastions of liberal thinking, but we must be more so in the future. Getting back to critical-thinking forms of teaching would be a good start. We need a plan to increase access, even as funds proposed for federal student support are whispered to be on the chopping block. We need to rethink what kinds of ideas can and should be heard on campuses. If we do not wish to be disregarded in the policy community, we need to think about how we can be heard in our communities, as public intellectuals, and how we can make ourselves heard as researchers in an unwelcoming environment. Action in the public sphere may be the only thing that saves our sanity, until the country as a whole regains its own composure. I would like to suggest several ways in which we can more forcefully insert ourselves into a national conversation, particularly with respect to our own research, but equally, explore what it means to "distribute" education as a social justice achievement. There are things we can do in public life and there are things we can do in our professional lives. Our professional lives are partially the focus of this work, but I would like to suggest that there are things to be done in our public lives that will count, too.

For instance, we can join public protests when they are in our towns and cities. We can write and phone our congressional representatives. Often, a postcard or an email will even get a response. Every message somehow counts.

We can volunteer somewhere in our towns and cities in agencies, nongovernmental organizations, and charities which strengthen communities. These kinds of efforts have the effect, I believe, of creating habits that are less likely to fall prey to authoritarian or totalitarian elements, and, at the same time, repel violence.

We can canvas for a political party.

We can give two hours to a phone bank for a progressive candidate.

We can join a respected group—for a small membership fee—which fights for environmental protections, such as the Sierra Club, Defenders of Wildlife, or other wildlife or conservation organizations that litigate for protection of wilderness areas, wildlife, endangered species, or national parks. The $25 a year this will cost you is quite small, but which, when added to the memberships of thousands or millions of others, provides a strong voice for defense of our natural heritage and critical biodiversity. Defending the wild and the wilderness is itself a form of resistance.

Professional Lives

There are actions we can take in our professional lives, too. In some ways, our professional lives are as private as many of us think our personal lives are. It is frequently only our colleagues and our "invisible colleges" who see, or know about, the work we do, whether it is teaching or research. Cloistered behind what many believe to be an "ivory tower," the public at large has little notion of what we do or what kinds of activities organize our days. It is why I refer to the resistance work we do in our communities as "public" and occasionally refer to our professional work as "private." Of course, in an era of surveillance capitalism, virtually nothing we do remains unrecorded, but nevertheless, some forms of resistance are more public, and some rather more performed away from the public eye, such as our teaching, our research, and our institutional and academic lives.

A caveat might be in order. It is clear we are living in parlous times. We confront a national administration that is not only indifferent, but is actively hostile to science and social science. It leads us to wonder whether anything we do will be taken into account, used for sane social or educational policy, or funded. A word of hope is appropriate here: No matter how desperate the times seem, or how intrusive or inhumane a neoliberal politic appears, things will change. While it would seem that no one is listening to our wisdom or attending to our serious social-science research, someone *is* listening. Maybe not right this moment, but things will change. We will be sane again. And our work will have some meaning again. So we have to keep working at it.

What do I mean by working at it? I mean two things. First, I mean we have to turn out qualitative and ethnographic work that is serious, rigorous, and compelling to a variety of audiences. This means that the work we do cannot be frivolous, or incomprehensible to serious audiences. It means that we may have to forgo, for the moment, some of the more far-flung theoretical and/or post-something work with which we are currently enamored. It means we have to concentrate on the quality of our work, including what some of my critics call *methodolatry*, serious concerns about method, about systematicity, about evidence (Lincoln & Guba, 1985; Guba & Lincoln, 1989; Lubet, 2018). Second, it means that qualitative research itself will need to reflect the transformed terrain of neoliberal, postneoliberal, and late capitalist regimes, encompassed by globalism and globalist organizational and governmental forms. It means qualitative research will need to look in unlikely places for data, evidence, and "connecting the dots." Some further explanation may be necessary.

The Context

It is likely the massive social changes of the past 15–20 years will filter into the practices and methods of qualitative research and contemporary ethnography. The pervasive effects of globalization, internationalization, corporatization, privatization of public goods, and ubiquitous social media are being felt at the most local, and even parochial, level (Westbrook, 2008). They are being felt keenly in higher and tertiary education, where institutions expand their reach to global audiences and students, where disciplines struggle to internationalize their curricula as well as their student recruitment, and where, increasingly, institutions operate more like entrepreneurial corporations than eleemosynary organizations. Massive *assemblages*, à la Deleuze and Guattari (1987, 2004), are being created from corporate-university-federal government complexes, the intricacies of which baffle much of even the long-term technical core, the faculty. Not surprisingly, such massive social changes are being felt equally strongly, if not as clearly, in private life as well. Shifts in the world of work from manufacturing to technology, information, and service industries have left some in the workforce with few, if any, skills to make smooth transitions from one form of economy to other, newer, forms, with concomitant displacement and joblessness for large sectors of the population.

As qualitative researchers seek to understand the changes they observe, their methods will have to take into account new formulations of some traditional methods. Documentary analysis, long a staple for studying complex organizations, will be replaced by requests for email records and memoranda stored in electronic files (if stored at all) or the cloud. Much of what we understand about institutions in the future will be linked to what has been saved from an era when email recipients are requested to not print out the message unless absolutely necessary. Qualitative researchers of the next century will need to be totally familiar with social media and with the possibilities and limits of collecting such artifacts (Facebook pages, websites, tweets, blogs, Instagrams, etc.) if they are to understand how, and on what information, institutional participants are acting. Such researchers are likely, too, to engage in *bricolage* to a greater extent, creating data sets from unlikely, disparate, and unaccustomed sources in order to comprehend some aspect of interest. Not coincidentally, researchers will have to deal with missing data (Lincoln, 2013)—data which are no longer available, or which are deliberately being withheld (Faubion & Marcus, 2009)—and will consequently have to rely more strongly on logical inferences regarding events. The more complex the organization, the more easily and readily it can conceal information it does not wish to have made public. The next generation of ethnographers of society and higher education will face both a richer and a less familiar and comprehensible set of organizations in which to study.

Given the diversifying and globalizing nature of society as well as postsecondary education, and given the necessity to invent methods beyond what has been considered the province of traditional qualitative research, three issues need to be taken into account. First, I would like to consider the methods themselves—what has been invented, what may yet be invented, and boundaries around and barriers to the latter. Second, I want to urge some cautions regarding new methods, both those that exist and those that have yet to be created or jerry-rigged. Finally, I want to proffer some teleological considerations about all of this world-yet-to-come/world-under-construction and what it can offer to a professional resistance toward encroaching authoritarianism, limits to academic freedom, societal pluralism, and other threats to democratic and socially just practices.

New Methods

Technology and globalization are reshaping the terrain of both society and postsecondary education. Consequently, when we think about new methods, technology comes first to mind, reminding us that there are efforts to move Western society (and perhaps the world) toward a "paperless" society. Some of what we might wish to examine will not exist in filing cabinets but perhaps be embedded on a hard drive, in email, in documents resting in "the cloud." Electronic access is both a blessing and a curse, because much of what we might want to access may not be readily available to us as researchers or may even be quietly withheld. More about that later. Most immediately, however, we need to think about social media, Second Life, avatars, LinkedIn, Facebook accounts, the millions of photographs and other visual media such as YouTube that are being created, stored, and sometimes treated as open access, that are now available to us. Depending on our need for some kinds of data, social media—particularly if we are looking, for example, at new students entering higher education—might provide us windows on the issues they face and give us direction for policy formulation.

We do not, insofar as I can tell, utilize the data that may be contained in blogs—which proliferate daily—to any great extent. The overwhelming array of data to which we have access makes the scholar's choice of what to use, and what to seek out, practically paralyzing, although it sharpens the need for asking increasingly pointed questions as a means for focusing our inquiries. Nevertheless, such data will add thick context to any social science studies we elect to undertake and will become a greater contributor to our studies in the future. Podcasts fall into this category as well. With growing frequency, regularly programmed television broadcasts are available 24/7 via podcasts, available on demand for anyone wishing to view or re-view them at some time other than their initial broadcast.

We will also need to ask about audiences, as some audiences will be persuaded by findings that tend to fit with their ontological dispositions, and others will be persuaded otherwise, by equally compelling senses of what is real and what matters, as well as how they learn about what matters. A portion of this is connected, I believe, to the current press for mixed methods, including not only a nod to the Cochrane Collaboration's (Grimshaw, Santesso, Cumpston,

Mayhew, & McGowan, 2006) definition of the "gold standard" (or clinical trial model) in research, but also a rising understanding that while experimental methods can tell you "what," they have no power to tell you "why," a task that qualitative methods performs elegantly.

Social media, blogs, and the world of information in cyberspace may provide us some answers to the whys and diverse perspectives that, for instance, new students, new faculty, and new administrators bring to newly configured, corporatist institutions or that new participants bring to their experiences with new corporate and globalized organizational forms.

Boundaries and Barriers to New Methods

There are, however, boundaries to the invention of new methods and methodological strategies. There are increasing concerns regarding privacy, and entrance into individuals' Facebook accounts, for instance, is typically controlled by the individual owner. Institutional Review Boards have yet to deal with researcher proposals that seek entrance into such social media, and researchers are left to negotiate such access with each individual account holder. How entrance is sought and obtained is as yet unregulated (and perhaps that is a good thing, given the intrusiveness of the IRB process as it stands now).

Larger problems, however, hover. In a world increasingly characterized by intricate, multinational, complex agreements, memoranda of understanding, networked relationships, layered fiscal arrangements, and Deleuzian *assemblages* between institutions of higher education, corporations and industry, and military organizations—the "global morass"—Westbrook (2008) points out that "for contemporary ethnography, the question is not destabilizing inherited categories, but establishing what the operative categories are" (p. 75). Indeed, the establishment of operative categories may prove to be the main accomplishment of an ethnographic undertaking. Once the categories are determined, the process confronting ethnographers of higher education is to locate and explicate the linkages between center and periphery. And it is the center which has received the least attention (Westbrook, 2008). Accessing that center—where decisions are being made, frequently without the slightest regard for shared governance—and prizing open the paths of power is not an easy task. Rather than confront that task, researchers have confined themselves to the margins, where they frequently study the "victims" of social process, including the disinherited of higher education. Perhaps we need to reconsider "studying up" again, examining where and how institutions are being reframed and reconstituted. Getting at the center, however, one confronts boundaries that effectively prevent access.

Cautions about New Methods

No one can talk about the invention of new methods without thinking about a concomitant problem: What constitutes rigor in the use of new methods? How do we establish systematicity and rigorous discipline when we access a chat room, an online community of interest, a set of personal Facebook accounts? We haven't worked out what the new methods are yet, let alone what constitutes rigorous use of new forms of data. It's not that we've worked out standard procedures for dealing with all interview data: classical, postmodern, or what-not. But we do know a tremendous amount about the interviewing process, and various authors have been stunningly insightful about interviewing's possibilities and limitations in the midst of the "interview society" (Kvale, 1996; Gubrium & Holstein, 2002; Fontana & Prokos, 2007). In the same vein, books and articles around utilizing the new media—online interviewing, use of social media, tapping into online chat rooms, and the like—are beginning to appear, with multiple real-life examples of how such cybermaterials have been utilized and how they might be used in the future (Markham, 1998; Markham & Baym, 2009).

Rubrics and metrics for judging the quality of such use—a set of criteria for using such data sources well, and for judging their accuracy and veracity, as well as their authenticity—are less available. We simply do not have the rules worked out well at the moment. Criteria for judging the rigor employed when utilizing virtual or cyber-materials are works in progress, still under development, and awaiting field testing and deep critique.

In the same vein, although I am aware that I have colleagues who believe that coding is bad, "mechanistic," and therefore should be avoided, there is nevertheless coding going on when such individuals speak of "chunks of data" (What constitutes a "chunk"? How is a "chunk" constituted?) (Jackson & Mazzei, 2012). Such coding may be implicit and tacit, but the very decision to "chunk" data is a decision to code. My point is that we don't have rules yet for coding the products of cyberspace. Conversations with researchers who inquire into online communities leads me to believe that some form of thematic analysis is carried over from traditional empirical materials, but few have commented on this matter. Currently, even with new empirical materials available to us from online communities and social media, we have no hard and fast rules for how they might be used most profitably. Many researchers simply treat such data as they would treat standard interview or observational data, with the proviso, of course, that there is no face-to-face interaction on which one might base judgments concerning the veracity of the construction, or even, on occasion, the gender of the speaker.

Consequently, while we have a universe of new forms of empirical materials available to researchers, and researchers are inventing ways and means of utilizing those materials, we still have no reliable means—save our own familiarity with the community—to ensure that what we are seeing/reading/viewing is what it purports to be. This reminds me of a recent television ad, where a young man and woman are in conversation, and he asks, "Where did you hear that?" Her reply is that she read it on the Internet, so of course it had to be true, right? Everything on the Internet is the truth ....

Despite my concerns about cautious use of some materials available to us from virtual modes, no doubt researchers will plow ahead, seeing what they can make of such work, and where and how it can and will be useful. It is the case, however, that we may find we are asking different questions of the digital data available to us. We may ask what it tells us not about an individual, but about social life, about collegiate life, about life increasingly diverse and pluralistic. We may ask where virtual worlds begin and end and where other forms of reality take over. We may ask how digital media come to substitute for face-to-face interactions and what that tells us about the work we need to do in classrooms to create real-life communities, real-life commitments, and real-life involvements, particularly with a growing disengagement with civic life. It's difficult to know, however, whether such work in its early stages will be found persuasive for policy purposes. As metrics for gauging the worth of such materials are invented, we may find that situation alters.

A Teleology of the New Qualitative Research

George Marcus posits that

> The widespread call today for a public ethnography (Marcus, 2005) already signals the intense interest of anthropologists in the responses to their work by the publics of varying composition and scale that it is able to touch. These responses matter more to many anthropologists, at least affectively, than professional responses to their work within the discipline, which I believe are weaker in intensity, and often less substantive, than sources of broader reception—both academic and nonacademic. (2009, p. 31)

Indeed, the externalization of the focus of higher education research toward the policy arena recognizes and honors the "call for a public ethnography," one which will be responsive to information needs of policy formulation communities but also responsive to the necessity to attend to issues of equity, access, and the redistribution of social goods toward more just ends. While higher education researchers have always been sensitive to the ways in which they found their research influencing policy—or hoping that it might do so—we have rarely in the academy focused our work on the policy community so forcefully, choosing rather to speak within the research community while we made quiet forays into policy circles when the opportunities arose. Increasingly, we are pointedly addressing state and federal policy units, speaking with both qualitative and quantitative empirical data, in an effort to attract attention from legislative bodies on behalf of higher education, potential students, K–12 education, and broader social landscapes. I believe we give congressional testimony more often, act as expert witnesses and *amici curiae*, participate in legal actions, write newspaper editorials and blogs, and work with foundations and advise think tanks more than at any time in the past.

In short, we are moving toward a public ethnography, conscious that our publics reach far beyond our own small academic community. The "ends" of ethnography that we envision are far broader than they were when many of us "old regime" folks entered the profession. The public ethnography toward which we are moving, however, has a different flavor from that which Marcus describes. It is far more desperate, far more critical, far more dangerous than any we have ever undertaken, if for no other reason than that the stakes are so much higher. The regime in which we work slides inexorably toward the authoritarian and fascist, as infants, toddlers, and children are caged without parents, powerful and well-funded forces are eager to strip the social safety net from millions of citizens, healthcare is treated as though it were a luxury for only those who can afford it, and naturalized citizens, guilty of no crime, are targeted for denaturalization and deportation. Because the times are so perilous, every research act is not merely a window toward knowledge; it is a conscious and courageous action toward resistance. When administration supporters jeer "Lock her up!" or threaten to shoot and kill "libtards," the threat level is escalating every day.

This should not surprise us. The Internet and other digital media have collapsed the world(s) we inhabit, permitting us to touch audiences and stakeholders in more immediate and pressing ways than were ever possible, but likewise, permitting hostile audiences to touch the primarily liberal professoriate with anonymous threats and the very real potential to do great harm. Consequently, our teaching is both more important and more delicate, our skills need buttressing in order to deal with "difficult dialogues" in the classroom in a fair and balanced manner, and our research needs to consciously sharpen its focus.

Conclusion

Thus, we have three considerations for qualitative methods in higher education for the 21st century: What sorts of methods will be available to us, and what are the methods not yet invented that we will be utilizing? What are the criteria we employ to assure that we are using the data in responsible, compelling, systematic, and disciplined ways? And how will our stakeholders and audiences expand in such a way as to extend the influence of our best research on policy, legislation, access, and equity?

As Sally Jackson (1986/2009) reminds us, "method is not a recipe for success, but a means of argument." Markham goes on to observe that

> The "steps taken" to solve a "problem" constitute method, but these steps are loaded with assumptions and premises before the process even begins. To understand and apply the appropriate method, one must also examine the guiding assumptions. Then, one must match the most

appropriate method to the question, retaining consistency among one's ontological, epistemological, and methodological premises." (p. xv)

Our questions for the 21st century will change, but it is up to us to assure that our answers are persuasive by maintaining consistency between and among the premises and assuring that we tilt toward the social justice that we see being eroded before our eyes. For the foreseeable future, our work has to be cast not only as a knowledge production activity, but also as a political act of resistance.

References

Bullock, A., & Trombley, S. (Eds.). (1999). *The Norton dictionary of modern thought.* New York, NY: W.W. Norton.

Deleuze, G., & Guattari, F. (1987). *A thousand plateaus: Capitalism and schizophrenia.* B. Massumi, trans. Minneapolis, MN: University of Minnesota Press.

Deleuze, G., & Guattari, F. (2004). *Anti-Oedipus: Capitalism and schizophrenia.* B. Massumi, trans. Minneapolis, MN: University of Minnesota Press.

Faubion, J.D., & Marcus, G.E. (Eds.). (2009). *Fieldwork is not what it used to be: Learning anthropology's method in a time of transition.* Ithaca, NY: Cornell University Press.

Fontana, A., & Prokos, A.H. (2007). *The interview: From formal to postmodern.* Walnut Creek, CA: Left Coast Press.

Grimshaw, J.M., Santesso, N., Cumpston, M., Mayhew, A., & McGowan, J. 2006, Winter). Knowledge for knowledge translation: The role of the Cochrane Collaboration. *Journal of Continuing Education in the Health Professions,* 26(1), 55–62.

Guba, E., & Lincoln, Y.S. (Eds.). (1989). *Fourth generation evaluation.* Newbury Park, CA: SAGE.

Gubrium, J.F., & Holstein, J.A. (Eds.). (2002). *Handbook of interview research: Context and method.* Thousand Oaks, CA: SAGE.

Jackson, A., & Mazzei, L. (2012). *Thinking with theory in qualitative research: Viewing data across multiple perspectives.* New York, NY: Routledge.

Jackson, S. (1986). Building a case for claims about discourse structures. In D.G. Ellis & W.A. Donohue (Eds.), *Contemporary issues in language and discourse processes.* (pp. 129–147). Hillsdale, NJ: Erlbaum.

Kvale, S. (1996). *InterViews: An introduction to qualitative research interviewing.* Thousand Oaks, CA: SAGE.

Lincoln, Y.S. (2013, May). *Dance-away data: To read/write from the hollows.* Paper presented at the annual meeting of the International Congress of Qualitative Inquiry, University of Illinois, Urbana.

Lincoln, Y.S., & Guba, E.G. (1985). *Naturalistic inquiry.* Thousand Oaks, CA: SAGE.
Lubet, S. (2018). *Interrogating ethnography: Why evidence matters.* New York, NY: Oxford University Press.
Marcus, G.E. (2005). *Multi-sited ethnography: Five or six things I know about it now.* Retrieved from eprints.ncrm.ac.uk/64/1/georgemarcus.pdf
Marcus, G.E. (2009). Notes toward an ethnographic memoir of supervising graduate research through anthropology's decades of transformation. In J.D. Faubion & G.E. Marcus (Eds.), *Fieldwork is not what it used to be: Learning anthropology's method in a time of transition* (pp. 1–35). Ithaca, NY: Cornell University Press.
Markham, A.N. (1998). *Life online: Researching real experience in virtual space.* Walnut Creek, CA: AltaMira Press.
Markham, A.N., & Baym, N.K. (Eds.). (2009). *Internet inquiry: Conversations about method.* Los Angeles, CA: SAGE.
Westbrook, D.A. (2008). *Navigators of the contemporary: Why ethnography matters.* Chicago, IL: University of Chicago Press.

Note

[1] When I use the term *teleology*, I reference the traditional philosophical meaning of the term. According to the *Norton Dictionary of Modern Thought* (Bullock & Trombley, 1999), teleology is "the study of ends, goals or purposes; more specifically, the theory that events can only be explained, and that evaluation of anything (objects, states of affairs, acts, agents) can only be justified, by consideration of the ends towards which they are directed" (p. 860).

CHAPTER FIVE

Shuffling the Deck
The "Woman Card," Misogyny, and Material-Discursive Complicatings of "Identities"

Janet L. Miller

PRE-2016 PRESIDENTIAL ELECTION: Incessantly checking news feeds on my phone; arriving minutes late to meetings because of "breaking news" updates; succumbing to nightly channel-surfing frenzies comparing Nate Silver's "Hillary" poll numbers with others' projections. In the early morn of November 8th, donning a white suffragette-inspired scarf, reviewing directions to my just-recently-changed voting location in West Harlem, joining in the chatter punctuating our surging-out-the-door voting queue, scanning my phone to find video clips of those in Rochester, New York, who were placing their "I Voted" stickers on the grave of suffragette leader Susan B. Anthony.

POST-2016 ELECTION: Still living—as I have for three decades now—in a city that has not voted for a Republican since Ronald Reagan in 1984. New York—a city that, in large if not total part, relishes continuing exposings of Trump's racist, xenophobic, and sexist work practices; that disdains the gaudy edifices that display his name across the cityscape; that detests his incessant disparagings and debasings, not just of Hillary Rodham Clinton—"that nasty woman"—but also of Mexicans, Muslims, the disabled, migrants, a "Gold Star" mother, refugees, First Nations people, all "politically correct" academics, football playing and kneeling among other actions, African-Americans, environmentalists, persons who claim homo-, trans-, or nonbinary sexualities, a U.S. Senator and decorated war hero who endured capture and torture, the poor, "elite" East and West coast citizens ... on and on and on.

DAILY CHALLENGINGS: Attempting—but most often failing—to ignore prolonged media dissections of both Hillary's and others' versions of "what happened." Flinching, not just the first time, but every time I hear the word "president" attached to his name; muting the audio almost every time he opens his mouth. January 21, 2017: Stomping up Fifth Avenue in the Women's March, shouting, chanting, becoming massive undulating ribbons, weaving together in simultaneous shock, outrage, and clenched-teeth determinations, unfurling a collective resolve. Focusing not only on expressing horror and indignation, but also on naming as well as working against multiple negative effects of this president's daily tweetings filled with misstatements, self-aggrandizements, and vicious denigrations of any and all who dare to "disagree," any and all whom he and his followers classify and reject as "other."

Multiplicities of Tensions

Unleashings of virulent misogynist, racist, homophobic, and xenophobic attacks during and following the 2016 U.S. presidential election—taking place on U.S. streets *and* in schools nationwide—are impelling myriad education-focused qualitative inquirers' research studies. Many such projects, proliferating especially in relation to effects of veiled, literal, symbolic, and normative violences, are building upon and expanding the work of critical qualitative researchers who have been and continue to be "profoundly engaged with issues of race, gender and socioeconomic levels as major shapers as well as components of historically reified structures of oppression, [including] whiteness, ... imperialist forms of power ... [and] relations shaped by conquest and occupation" (Cannella & Lincoln, 2015, p. 246).

And indeed, late on the evening of November 8, 2016, as election results were cementing the fact of Trump's win, CNN commentator Van Jones spoke of "whitelash" against a diversified country and a Black president as a major reason for Hillary's defeat. Jones detailed aspects of that whitelash in what he called "the nightmare" that literally was unfolding during his live broadcast, relaying that Muslim friends as well as members of terrified immigrant families were texting him, asking if they should leave the country. But of course and for brief example, varied U.S.-centered historical analyses have focused on earlier examples of numerous backlashes, including the long Jim Crow era that followed Reconstruction—an "era" that has not yet ended, according to many, including civil rights lawyer and legal scholar Michelle Alexander's (2010) analyses of the "new Jim Crow." Historians also have noted the rise of the religious right in response to further racist as well as antifeminist sentiments that followed the potent, although never unitary, Civil Rights and Women's Movements (Blake, 2012, 2016). However, Van Jones's naming of whitelash in its most current and virulent forms, among other critiques and examinations of the 2016 U.S. presidential election, has contributed to even more direct and concomitant attention to all "structures of oppression" with which critical qualitative education researchers, along with innumerable others, have long been grappling.

But post-2016 presidential election, Hillary Rodham Clinton, although clearly recognizing multiple interactions, complexities, and enduring oppression structures that may have affected the election outcome, specifically and repeatedly has identified misogyny as a major contributing factor to her devastating loss. Her particular naming of such may well be impelled by what the editors of *The New Yorker* (The Choice, 2016), in their stirring endorsement of her candidacy, noted—that is, Hillary "has been the target of 25 years of hatred, misogyny, and conspiracy-mongering, endlessly metamorphosing from one confected 'scandal' to another—Filegate, Benghazi, the State Department emails" (p. 35).

Obviously, such observations have joined in propelling several of my entwined reasons for choosing to consider here varied iterations and effects of misogyny and "the woman card," as both played by and dealt to Hillary. Although much theorizing in recent decades has decentered humanist assumptions of "the self" and any attendant essentializations of "identity" categories, the ongoing, dramatic and too-often now violent effects of misogyny, racism, homophobia, and xenophobia are demanding critical analyses and actions to prevent further and accelerating incidents born of "historically reified structures of oppression." I thus focus here on "misogyny," in particular, as a word, a concept, a result that we cannot retire (Pillow, 2018) because it signals actions that emanate from historically oppressive assumptions about and actions against women, writ large. And obviously, #Me Too, #Time's Up, and #Say Her Name, alongside the Black Lives Matter and Never Again movements, are impelling current critical analyses and actions against subordinating and too-often-abusive acts directed toward all those deemed "other, less than." But I also here specifically center the 2016 election and Hillary's loss because of long-time entanglings with feminisms across my own curriculum theorizing and qualitative inquiries that have and continue to interrogate issues and conceptualizations of gender, especially in relation to the prominent, always contingent and contentious identity category of "woman"—of "woman" teacher, researcher, writer, in particular (for example, see Miller, 1990; 2005; 2017).

Obviously, my own researching predilections, including my theoretical positionings, are those chosen from among widely differing beliefs and theoretical stances. And even within any one stance and positioning are multiply complicating and often irresolvable tensions. For example, I wholeheartedly continue to support contingently situated needs, desires, and actions in relation to forms of "identity politics" that enable struggles for and attainment of human rights. Current and escalating normative and literal violences occurring far too regularly in neighborhoods and schools across the United States literally compel what I concur are necessarily "identity"-based and -driven political movements and actions.

Concurrently, however, assumptions of unitary-only versions of "identities"—already theoretically complicated by decades of decenterings of the subject that now instead position the them-I, the cis-I, the non-I, the queer-I, the crip-I, the post-I—just to mention a few—seem to me overwhelmingly inadequate in light of current and proliferating complexities of subjectivities, including those who refuse binary-only assumptions about gender and race, for example. At the very least, then, I remain convinced by queer feminist philosopher Judith Butler's (1992) contention that any named identity, if so claimed as necessary and desired or as assigned, still must be understood and lived as that which "designates an undesignatable field of differences, one that cannot be totalized or summarized by a descriptive identity category, [and thus] the very term becomes a site of permanent openness and resignifiability" (p. 160).

But clearly, daily denials, rejections, and acts of hatred toward such permanently open and resignifying potentialities are appearing with increasing velocity, not only in the United States, but also worldwide. Thus, I'm considering that critical qualitative inquirers, working with and in constantly spewing tensions generated by contemporary contexts as well as vastly complicating theoretical perspectives, may well want to think about possibly responding in ways that recall Lather's (1995) caution: "As critical practices derive their forms and meanings in relation to their changing historical conditions, positions of resistance can never be established once and for all. They must, instead, be perpetually refashioned to address adequately the shifting conditions and circumstances that ground them" (pp. 167–168).

Shifting Conditions and Circumstances ...

I therefore quickly float here some possible versions of resistance-refashioning efforts that might be extrapolated from what Elizabeth St. Pierre (2011) has conceptualized and named as "post qualitative research." Of course, current examples of "post" inquiries (Lather & St. Pierre, 2013; MacLure, 2013, 2015; St. Pierre, 2013, 2014; Lather, 2016; St. Pierre, Jackson, & Mazzei, 2016) have been greatly informed by theorizings and studies that presaged post qualitative studies. Albeit with varying emphases and situated concerns, earlier works that gestured toward what now are termed post research iterations both signaled and responded to "changing historical conditions" (see, for example: Guba, 1990; Lather, 1991, 1993; Davies, 1993, 2000; Cannella, 1997; Denzin, 1997; Lincoln, 1998; Denzin & Lincoln, 2000; St. Pierre & Pillow, 2000; Pillow, 2003; Guba & Lincoln, 2005; Hammersley, 2008; Tamboukou, 2008). They did so by wrestling especially with myriad influences of sociocultural and theoretical shifts that challenged standard qualitative research assumptions about methodologies, as well as issues of representation, for example. Such responsive qualitative scholarship *in fact* had to contend with multiple mid- to late-20th-century discursive and material variations that were and continue to be promulgated by what typically are identified as the postmodern, narrative, linguistic, postcolonial, poststructural, and ontological "turns," among others. Indeed, for some time now, qualitative researchers have been attending to implications of such "turns," even as they differently prioritize intentions and commitments. For example,

> the emancipatory turn organized around the identity categories that enabled feminist, race-based, queer, social justice, and postcolonial critiques—liberatory critiques—aimed at combating

oppression. The postmodern and poststructural turns were also deeply concerned with ethics and deconstructing and opening up oppressive material-discursive structures. (St. Pierre, Jackson, & Mazzei, 2016, p. 101)

Further, and in relation to overarching concerns taken up by post qualitative researchers, current iterations of what are often termed "the new materialisms and new empiricisms" also clearly build upon but also challenge varied aspects of the turns. For example, some now offer multiple angles of interrogation on how life might be understood without privileging the sovereign category of *human*, or of any essentialized identity concept, such as "woman," or of even the very notion of "the self." Versions of new materialist, affect, and posthuman critical humanities in fact dispute and reject not only unitary, singular, autonomous, essentialized versions of "identities," but also of "humans" that supposedly possess sovereign, separate, and dominant status as living entities. Karen Barad's (2007) well-known examinations of the nature of discursive practices, for example, allow a focus on how discursive practices are related to material phenomena as well as on how, *lacking* "an independent, self-contained existence ... individuals emerge through and as a part of their entangled intra-relating," (p. ix).

From another angle on such issues, posthumanism, conceived in part as a social discourse (in the Foucauldian sense), negotiates the pressing question of what it means to be human as especially entangled conditions of globalization, technoscience, late capitalism, and climate change. So, the "critical" in the "critical posthumanities" also now gestures toward complicated and nondialectical relationships between the human and the posthuman as well as their respective dependence on the nonhuman (Braidotti & Hlavajova, 2018). Post qualitative inquiries, writ large, then, may well include new materialist conceptualizings of "woman not as a masculine defined body, but as a phenomenon produced by language, science, technology, and apparatuses ... [and therefore] not as foundational or oppositional, but as the product of an array of factors not limited to language" (Hekman, 2014, p. 159).

Concurrent questions focus on how/might such theorizings enable simultaneous wrestlings with aggressive unravellings of equitable and humane conditions and rights for all lively matter—issues which currently remain prominent for most versions of critical qualitative research. How/might education researchers explore circulations of intensities in these unravelings wherein "identities" emerge via their entanglements, thus "becoming" embodied engagements with materialities of research data (Taguchi, 2013), for example? Such explorations *can* be part of the fight against the appearance of new planes of discrimination and their destructive consequences.

However, such issues, questionings, and perspectives *do* necessitate, in particular, difficult wrestlings with widely differing rethinkings of the nature of being as well as of perspectives on how we come to know, not to mention what and whose knowledges, as well as very "beings," are deemed "of most worth." But continuing ponderings of varied perspectives about ontology, epistemology, and the very conceptualizing and "doings" of qualitative research are imperative aspects of enacting not just post but all versions of qualitative research as "*ethico*-onto-epistemological project[s] [that call for] heightened curiosity and accompanying experimentations" (St. Pierre, Jackson, & Mazzei, 2016, p. 100) in the conceptualizings and "becomings" of existence.

Such calls are based upon post qualitative researcher perspectives that align with the "new materialisms/empiricisms" and their interrogatings of poststructural/postcolonial thought as always privileging the linguistic over the material. Rather than rejecting crucial postfoundational insights, however, these "new" materialisms offer reasons for bringing the ontological into such "posts" efforts to greatly trouble the reified discourse/reality binary. Such ontologically oriented perspectives thus work to incite projects that not only make evident ways that language *alone* does *not* construct reality, but also embrace "the material [in a way that] acknowledges and builds on the insights of linguistic constructionism" (Hekman, 2014, p. 148). In so doing, work such as Barad's (2007), for example, focuses on the nature of discursive practices by examining how such practices are related to all material phenomena.

Judith Butler, although serving as a target for some new materialists who critique her work as only focused on the discursive, has expanded and deepened her theorizing of "performativity" (1990, 2004a, 2004b, 2009, 2015a, 2015b) by arguing that performative effects may become material effects and all are part of the processes of materialization.

Butler indeed offers an account of ontological effects that enable rethinkings of the very conceptualizations and embodiments of materiality itself. According to Butler, all the elements that figure into subjectivity, then, have both discursive and material components, none of which can be isolated and analyzed apart from the others. Butler's extensive work on precarity, for example, embodies explicit recognition of the material: As material beings, we all are variously precarious, dependent upon particular and situated political and social norms for our very material existences. Thus, one of Butler's primary concerns centers on the ethics surrounding who is and who is not recognized as possessing a grievable life—that is, who is recognized, or not, as a subject who possess an ontology, a being. Indeed, as feminist scholar Susan Hekman (2014) notes, "for subjects, the connection between the discursive and the ontological is more intimate than that of any other entity. Subjects can only 'be' within a discursive realm that grants them an ontology. Trying to understand how this operates is a uniquely difficult theoretical task" (p. 182).

Judith Butler indeed has pointed to such entanglings and their ethical implications:

> We might reread "being" as precisely the potentiality that remains unexhausted by any particular interpellation. Such a failure of interpellation may well undermine the capacity of the subject to "be" in a self-identical sense, but it may also mark the path toward a more open, even more ethical kind of being, one of or for the future. (1997, p. 131)

Such recognition of inexhaustible variations of being and becoming, for example, thus may also include theorizings of subjectivity as what feminist philosopher Rosi Braidotti (2018) speaks of as transspecies efforts that take place

> transversally, *in-between* nature/technology; male/female; black/white; local/global; present/past—in assemblages that flow across and displace the binaries. These in-between states defy the logic of the excluded middle .... Poststructuralism paved the way for this approach, but the posthuman turn materializes it and composes a new ontological framework of becoming-subjects. (p. 3)

Braidotti clearly does argue for a diversified and always-changing array of perceptions and formations of the "human" in the posthuman era as part of what she names as the work of the "critical posthumanities." But her view still recognizes difficulties posed by persistent iterations of binary "identity" constructions and their supposedly "natural" characteristics. Braidotti elaborates on persistent as well as current and multiplying ethical complexities of and challenges to the "we" of current transspecies efforts: "the dwellers of this planet at this point in time—are interconnected, but also internally fractured. Class, race, gender and sexual orientations, age and able-bodiedness continue to function as significant markers in framing and policing access to normal 'humanity'" (Braidotti, 2018, p. 23). Thus, Braidotti argues for what she names as critical cartographies that

> entail creativity ... in the process *of learning to think differently about ourselves* [my emphasis], in response to the complexity of our times. The aim of an adequate cartography is to bring forth alternative figurations or conceptual personae for the kind of knowing subjects currently constructed. All figurations are localized and hence immanent to specific conditions; for example, the nomadic subjects, or the cyborg, are not mere metaphors, but material and semiotic signposts for specific geo-political and historical locations. As such, they express grounded complex singularities, not universal claims. (Braidotti, 2018, p. 4)

At the same time, however, feminist scholar Leigh Gilmore (2012) notes that feminist and postcolonial theorists, for years now, have been performing what could be called posthumanist critiques. They have done so, in particular, not only by destabilizing, decentering the humanist subject as autonomous, unitary, and rational, but also by expanding "the human" as incorporating technological, collective, environmental, ecological as well as material features and mobilities. And Sidonie Smith (2012), feminist scholar of autobiographical studies, argues that such "early posthumanist" critiques also bear "witness to experiential histories of radical violence, degradation, and survival [that] involve negotiating categories of the human, in their ontological, political, and intersubjective dimensions" (p. 141).

I too briefly am gesturing here toward just a few of the myriad contemporary complexities that affect all aspects of living and researching in and with postanthropocentrism and its indeterminacies as well as with post qualitative research challenges and implications in mind. In quite limited ways, I've thus offered only slight glimpses into some current theorizing that is influencing what might be thought and learned in terms of "thinking differently about ourselves" as well as about our qualitative research assumptions and practices. Such "thinkings" of course gesture toward massive complexities and challenges posed by post qualitative research perspectives that, for example, reject the static, hierarchical logic of representation as well as practices of interpretation and analysis as conventionally understood (MacClure, 2013).

But I've pointed, albeit in a deeply truncated manner, to these myriad conundrums and intricacies because I specifically desire multiple interrogations of Hillary Rodham Clinton's presidential election defeat. I continue to push for such analyses, wondering if—and if so, how—complicatings and "undoings" of unitary implications of "human" and its supposedly attached and fixed "identities" that include iterations of "woman," "misogyny,", and "the woman card" might contribute to possible reshapings of positions of resistance within these contingent historical moments.

In relation to my focus here, such efforts could involve myriad reshufflings of the always-the-same deck of identity cards and all that it represents, for example. Because, in fact, reshapings of all kinds of assumptions and practices, including those of resistance as contextualized in nonviolent critical qualitative research, *necessarily* involve, at the very least, reshufflings that refuse assumptions that deal out only unitary presumptions of "identities" and their "meanings."

So, yes, I'm detailing my desires here to conjure versions of a deck that scatters and proliferates post material-discursive coconstitutive complexities and multiplicities—not only in relation to the category of *woman* but also in relation to potential refashionings of resistance in critical qualitative inquiries. But of course, my wishes are curtailed by all kinds of limitations, not only those of space, in this single chapter. The refashionings of positions of resistance that I point to here involve only initial forays into "mini" creatings and experimentings with critique, in particular, as a still-vital aspect of "learning to think differently about ourselves."

Refashionings ...

Indeed, research and analyses of historical precursors, contemporary situated iterations, and critiques of all current concerns I've briefly detailed—and more—*have and continue to be* a major focus for education researchers. Engaging in such work, I continue to hold in mind that, as Foucault posited and as Lather extrapolated, a critical analysis of one particular historical moment—of "self/identity" or of what and who might constitute "the human, nonhuman, posthuman," for example—*cannot* be considered as or simply result in "a permanent body of knowledge that is accumulating" (Foucault, 1984, p. 50) Instead, the epistemological *and* ontological work that Foucault called "critical" must be "conceived as an attitude, an ethos, a philosophical life in which the critique of what we are is at one and the same time the historical analysis of the limits that are imposed on us and an experiment with the possibility of going beyond them" (Foucault, 1984, p. 50).

For Foucault (1988), then, "the historical" is contingent, and critique is "not a matter of saying that things are not right as they are. It is a matter of pointing out on what kinds of assumptions, [on] what kinds of familiar, unchallenged, unconsidered modes of thought the practices we accept rest" (p. 154). Further, as Lather (1995) urges "refashionings," and as MacClure (2015) prods me toward critique as "immanent," as already caught up in processes and movements in which it is entangled, Foucault (1988) again reminds me: After identifying and questioning assumptions of that which has been constructed and reified into the taken-for-granted in certain historical moments, "one can no longer think things as one formerly thought them, [and] transformation becomes both very urgent, very difficult, and quite possible" (1988, p. 155).

Certainly, the current and widespread efforts embodied in the resurfaced #MeToo movement, as well as in #Time's Up, #Say Her Name, Black Lives Matter, and student-generated antigun protests across the United States—among many other equally vital concerns—are having profound effects, including no longer being able to "think things as one formerly thought them." These "things" include, for me, those conceptions and issues of gender and of the category *woman* that now compel refashionings, with experimentings with possibilities of and with my critical qualitative researcher attention, responses, and resistances. Continuing to be persuaded of the impossibilities *and* undesirabilities of positioning "gender" as a disconnected and autonomous category, I attempt, in my mini-experimentings, to consider implications of varied "woman" and "gender" constructions and assumptions, but not only in relation to the 2016 election. I also do so toward reshapings of critical qualitative research resistance positionings to continue "to plumb the archaeology of taken-for-granted perspectives to understand how unjust and oppressive social conditions came to be reified as historical 'givens'" (Cannella & Lincoln, 2015, p. 244).

Here, then, are just a few reminders (not that you need them) of pre- and postelection contentions, accusations, defenses, and laudings that represent varied and quite often dichotomous political stances as well as epistemological and ontological assumptions about Hillary Rodham Clinton as "woman":

- the first woman to be nominated by one of the two major political parties in the United States;

- the woman who, because her Whiteness and middle–upper-class status supply privilege while her "femaleness" conveys oppression, is an oppressor of others, even as she is oppressed herself;

- the woman who, as a scintillating intellectual pioneer throughout her career, was defeated by "a cartoonish misogynist" who "flaunted his contempt for women generally and for her, personally, even prowling behind her in a nationally televised debate" (Remnick, 2017, p. 32);

- the first woman who had a genuine chance to become the U.S. president;

- a woman who both articulates and obfuscates an "imperial feminism" (Eisenstein, 2016) that remains primarily White and privileged rather than explicitly multiracial and multiclass;

- a woman "not easily reduced to one transcendent myth," an "idealist and liberal incrementalist, a glass-ceiling-smashing lawyer and a cautious establishmentarian, a wife and mother, a First Lady, a rough-and-tumble political operator, a senator, a Secretary of State" (The Choice, 2016, p. 33).

These critiques and assessments, among myriad others, offer differing glimpses into the reiterative persistence—as well as damaging and too-often-now violent effects—of multiple binaries, those socially constructed and maintained dichotomies surrounding still-dominant and bifurcated conceptions of gender, race, class, sexuality, ethnicity, age, abilities, who and what counts as human, for brief examples. And of course, then, the very concepts of misogyny and "the woman card" imply what many have long critiqued as essentialized assumptions about any identity category, including biology-reified and binary-only versions of "woman" and "man," for example.

But assumptions of unitary "identities" and the binaries that historically have maintained the lesser status of the lesser, the "other" side, of the dominant construction—that is, "man/woman; mind/body; human/nature," for typical examples—seem increasingly inadequate in light of current and proliferating complexities of subjectivities, including those who daily live and refuse binary-only assumptions about gender and race, among many others. For example, well-known arguments against making ontological judgments about which genders should be considered "authentic" include those made by Judith Butler (2004b). Butler argues that any assumption of a singular, "authentic" version of "gender" perpetrates a form of "dehumanizing violence" upon genders that are disregarded, disdained, rejected.

But as noted, Hillary Rodham Clinton (2017), now out of the woods (with some, even in her own political party, now wishing that she'd return there), herself has named misogyny, specifically, as one of the major contributing factors to her devastating loss—even as her fellow Democratic opponent, Bernie Sanders, relentlessly argued that it was not sufficient to vote for Hillary just because she was a woman.

And amidst all the campaigning frenzies, former Secretary of State Madeleine Albright vehemently defended her words that implied there was a hellacious place awaiting women who don't support one another, a contention that immediately set social media ablaze with both criticism and support. Albright fortified her statement in a *Time* magazine interview (Newton-Small, 2016), saying that, "People need to understand who has been really fighting on behalf of issues that are of interest to women" (n.p.). Albright worried that many do not realize, in fact, the decades of struggles that have contributed to "get us here to this presidential possibility," and she cautioned that "we all have to remember that no matter what age we are, we can't go back" (n.p.).

But at the same time, for many, Albright's "in hell" statement purports to understand *the* issues that *all* women (universalized, essentialized way too often still as White, mostly middle-class women) face, even as Albright intended her comment to both highlight and garner support for Clinton's decades-long work as a "true fighter for women's rights" (Newton-Small, 2016, n.p.).

Indeed, varied analyses have and continue to emphasize differing angles on conceptions as well as impacts of misogyny on the 2016 election results, including those in relation to education and qualitative research (see, among others, Childers, 2017; Lather, 2017). And, of course, numerous academics from disciplinary and transdisciplinary orientations as well as journalists, nonfiction writers, and literary critics have offered myriad perspectives. Discussing her own surprise at her now-fiercely supportive sentiments about Hillary Clinton and what seemed for so long her possible election as the first woman president of the United States, a self-professed left-leaning academic, Judith Grant (2018), notes:

> There has been a profound double standard at work in the treatment of Hillary Clinton as a candidate. She has been despised and reviled not for any wrongs she has actually done but for accusations conjured to play into misogynist narratives of the unlikeable, power-hungry, conniving woman.... Despite the massive gerrymandering, despite the Russian hacking, Clinton still received 65,844,610 votes, almost three million more votes than Trump, and more votes than any candidate for president has ever received except Barack Obama.... She won 94% of black women and 68% of Latinas, who may not have voted for her because she is a woman, as Bernie Sanders implied, but rather because they did not care that she was a woman. The intersection of race and gender in 2016 is remarkable. It is as though the racism against Barack Obama combined with the misogyny against Hillary Clinton into some kind of one-two punch, leaving us with Donald Trump. (n.p.)

Further, Susan Bordo, professor of gender and women's studies at the University of Kentucky and Pulitzer Prize winner, argues that throughout Hillary's career, she has been "a living Rorschach test of people's nightmare images of female power" (2017a, p. 27). In *The Destruction of Hillary Clinton*, Bordo (2017a) details the escalation of vicious attacks on all aspects of Hillary's being; for example, in the 2008 campaign, posters hoisted against her demanded that Hillary "Iron my Shirts" and "Make Me a Sandwich." By 2016, posters pictured her on a broomstick, and crowds—egged on by HIM and his "Crooked Hillary" claims—regularly chanted, "Put the bitch in jail, lock her up."

Even with this escalated viciousness, however, many dismissed sexism as one viable reason for Hillary's "destruction"—and accused her and her followers of "playing the woman card." These dismissers and accusers included some who considered women's issues passé, thus ignoring major crises around reproductive rights and equal pay, to name just a very few, that Trump's election has indeed not only reinscribed but also escalated. Others, conceptualizing Hillary as the "lesser of two evils" or the "corporate whore," seemed almost benign in their critiques when juxtaposed with those who claimed that her vote alone was responsible for the Iraq War, that she ran and participated in a child pornography ring, engaged in animal sacrifice, and was a member of a feminist coven (Bordo, 2017a).

Among many similar misogynous attacks are those that have been directed at France's First Lady, Brigitte Macron, who is 24 years older than her husband, France's youngest-ever elected president. She was 39 and married with three children, when he, as a 15-year-old student, registered for her drama class in the school where she taught Latin, French, and drama. The French First Lady, characterized as both a "cougar" and a "grandmother" and the president as her "boy toy," for example, continues to suffer heated misogynous and ageist denigrations. However, some do note that these still appear somewhat "milder" (but notice the persistent hierarchical, competitive, and stereotypic assumptions that permeate the "woman" category, in particular) than those hurled at Hillary as early as 1978, when she assumed her role as First Lady of Arkansas.

But Hillary, like many others now especially encouraged and supported by the current version of #MeToo, among other vital worldwide movements, continues to refuse to retreat or to be silent in the face of such misogynous attacks (Bordo, 2017b). Indeed, like Hillary, Macron, and many others, esteemed Canadian writer Margaret Atwood refuses to accept the world only as it *permits*. Such refusals have encouraged Atwood to imagine the world as it might be. Atwood is described, in *The New Yorker* (Mead, 2017), as "the prophet of dystopia," and her 1985 novel, *The Handmaiden's Tale*, has received renewed and rapt attention as well as awards for its ongoing television serialization on Hulu.

Writing in *USA Today*, Atwood (2017, p. 3D) notes: "I put nothing into [the book] that has not been done in history at some time, in some place.... I didn't intend it to be prescient, I intended it to be a warning." And in the April 17, 2017, *New Yorker* interview, Atwood in fact stated that she believes what feels most disturbingly familiar to current viewers, readers, and rereaders of *The Handmaiden* is "... the blunt misogyny of the society" that [she] portrays. Atwood points to such "blunt misogyny" as that "which Trump's vocal repudiation of 'political correctness' has loosed into common parlance today" (p. 41).

Atwood's feminism, like Hillary's, assumes women's rights to be human rights. Atwood's convictions are grounded in "having been raised with a presumption of absolute equality between the sexes ... [that yielded what she calls] a critical distance on codes of femininity—an ability to see those codes as cultural practices worthy of investigation, not as necessary conditions to be accepted unthinkingly" (Mead, 2017, p. 43). Atwood posits that those who have scorned and skewered Hillary during the 2016 election—and certainly Trump's continuing vilification of her, most often still referring to her as "crooked Hillary" and supporting Fox News mandates that she be impeached (proof, Hillary jokingly contends, that both Trump and his main mouthpiece indeed seem to *think* that she *is* the president) actually might be more "explicable" when seen through the lens of the Puritan witch-hunts. "You can find websites that say Hillary was actually a Satanist with demonic powers," Atwood notes. Concomitantly, then, Atwood argues, with the Trump election, women have been put on notice that hard-won rights may only be provisional. "It's the return to patriarchy .... You're going to have ... [a] lot more dead women, a lot more illegal abortions, a lot more families with children in them left without a mother. They want it 'back to the way it was.' Well, *that is* part of the way it was" (Mead, 2017, pp. 41–42).

Some argue that evidence of such "backward" thinking also can be found in the "fact" that a majority (53%) of White women voted for Trump. According to certain analysts, these White women were uniquely positioned to protect *or* disrupt male White privilege and power—but apparently, claim these same analysts, *all* these women chose White privilege over gender equality as retribution for the supposed denigration of working-class White men by "multicultural" forces, in particular.

And, Hillary is certainly a very powerful White, privileged woman. She is also a multiple-times recipient of misogynist statements and actions. As the #MeToo, #SayHerName, and #TimesUp movements continue to reveal, women *are* sexually violated, abused, oppressed *as* women, and gender *and* race remain as constructs that maintain their bifurcated assumptions of "best, most powerful, dominant" and "less than, other." And these assumptions continue to prevail, despite, for example, Judith Butler's (1990) well-known complicatings of gender as "performative," as a repetitive citation of normative roles that—because of language's slippages as well as differing and changing social, cultural, psychological, discursive and historical systems, contexts, and embodiments within which sexual/gendered identities attain their meanings—simultaneously *are* open to variation and deviation.

But of course, disruptions of those essentialized identities historically positioned as the post privileged were launched in the United States during the 1960s Women's Movement by Women of Color, by those labeled "disabled," by those who claimed themselves as lesbian, trans, and/or bisexual, for brief examples. All these and more argued that unitary versions of feminism such as those represented by what most often are called First and Second Wave feminisms, as well as theories emanating from those "waves," in fact "created unity only through a strategy of exclusion" (Butler, 2004b, p. 206) by primarily attending not only to a unitary categorical identity marker of "woman" positioned most often as White, middle- and upper-class, able-bodied, and heterosexual, but also by minimizing or ignoring complications provided by multiple iterations of race, class, ethnicity, age, and sexuality, for example. Such challenges too were articulated, albeit from differing angles and concerns, by Audre Lorde (1984), Gayatri Spivak (1988), Kimberle Crenshaw (1989), Donna Haraway (1991), and bell hooks (1992), among many others.

For brief examples: Specific addressings of such concerns appeared via Kimberle Crenshaw's (1989) articulations of "intersectionality," which she originally posited as a dynamic term of analysis rather than a noun of identity, especially in relation to entwined oppressive systems of discrimination. As a civil rights lawyer as well as an academic, Crenshaw's concerns centered and continue to focus on ways that Black women's historically inflected circumstances and contexts could be analyzed in the law *neither* by "race" as defined only in relation to Black men, *nor* by "gender" as primarily considered only via White women's experiences.

From critical angles on analyses of centuries of colonizing practices and assumptions, Gayatri Spivak (1988) intended her concept of "strategic essentialism" as a strategy to position "essential attributes" *not* as "natural," but rather as those that can be defined and articulated, by any one particular and situated "group," as constructs to be invoked when it is politically useful to do so. Spivak subsequently bemoaned various misappropriations of her strategy as simply reinscribing essentialist characteristics against which she was working. In "Bonding with Difference," (Spivak & Arteaga, 1995), an interview conducted with Alfred Arteaga, Spivak in fact claimed that she has given up on the phrase, although not the concept.

And from entirely different angles, Donna Haraway's introduction of the concept "cyborg" as metaphor for disarticulating human/nonhuman as well as technological/social binaries indeed shattered assumptions of the body/human as an organic totality with a "natural" essence and "identity," against which difference is constructed as incompleteness or "less than," for example.

Judith Butler's (2015a, 2015b; Butler & Athanasiou, 2013) more recent theorizings continue as well as greatly elaborate and extend her engagements with such concerns, especially as she now focuses on effects of dispossession, precariousness, and the rights and potential power of "public assembly" in forging embodied coalitions and "identities" that momentarily coalesce and simultaneously "undo," that morph and shift, multiply and change. As I've already noted, then, Butler thus now also conceives "the subject," in general, not as a fundamental structure of being, but rather as entailing material *and* discursive components that cannot be isolated and analyzed apart from the others. Responding to her critics who argue that she has encapsulated these concepts only into the realms of the symbolic and the linguistic, Butler argues that engagement with an "other"—whether discursively *and* materially positioned as "the same" or as different—as liminal, as monstrous, as nonhuman, inhuman, an inert thing, as precarious—is always in relation with the social, very broadly defined as well as differently enacted and acted upon. *These* are the contingencies that usher *subjectivity* into being, Butler argues, including multiple variations on "woman," for obvious example.

At the same time, Butler (2017; Butler & Berbee, 2017; Chaillan, 2018) continues to grapple with pervasive essentialisms that still permeate reified identity categories and enactments, such as those evidenced in the 2016 election:

> Trump takes up space on the screen, becomes a looming figure, and this was brought out well by the "Saturday Night Live" sketch in which Alec Baldwin roams around the stage, appearing to almost attack Hillary. That kind of looming and threatening power draws, as well, on Trump's practices of sexual harassment. (2017, n.p.)

Butler further notes: "What should not be underestimated is the deep-seated rage and anger against Hillary, partially the result of a rank misogyny *and* the revulsion against Obama, fueled by long simmering racism." Similar to but further complicating in multiple ways Atwood's observations, Butler argues that, among many other assaults,

> Trump has unleashed pent up anger against feminists, [unitarily] figured as censorious police; against multiculturalism, [unitarily] viewed as a threat to white privileges; against migrants [unitarily] figured as a security threat .... For a world that is increasingly *mis*characterized as post-racial and post-feminist [with *post* here signaling the "after"—unlike "the past-future-present" of "the posts" of postcolonial, poststructural, new materialist, and posthuman thought], we are now seeing how misogyny and racism overrides judgment and a commitment to democratic and inclusive goals— they are sadistic, resentful, and destructive passions driving our country." (Butler & Berbee, 2017, n.p.)

At the same time, Butler notes, among the important contributions of "#MeToo," is the grasping by "the larger public [of] the systemic and pervasive existence of coercive sexual conduct against women [and its] taken-for-granted character .... The efforts to hystericize women who tell the story, who make the complaint, are no longer quite plausible" (Chaillan, 2018, n.p.). Butler's analyses of the 2016 election thus also attend to her constant recognition of tensions generated by contingently situated needs for "identity politics" in terms of fighting for and attaining rights, while simultaneously acknowledging what she, as I previously noted, for decades now has postulated as vital and *potentially generative* complicatings of any universalized "identity" assumptions—of "woman," for example, as necessarily signifying an "undesignatable field of differences" and thus as one "site of permanent openness and resignifiability" (1992, p. 160).

But in further contemplating contemporary U.S. contexts in relation to the 2016 election and the resulting violences—including the killing of one citizen in Charlottesville, Virginia, who was among those protesting peacefully against the White supremacists marching through that town—Butler (2017) makes an additional observation that I believe can further bolster critical qualitative researchers' work toward nonviolent forms of resistance and action. She notes:

> I see on my campus, for instance, that there are students who oppose racism by any means necessary. I want to oppose racism as well, but I do think it is worth pausing to ask by what means? If the means are violent, how are they justified? I would like to persuade people who are in righteous rage that the turn to violence is not what they finally want, since at stake is not just finding a way to react immediately and legibly but building a world together ... [and] to honor the obligation to affirm the life of another even if I am overwhelmed with hostility.... [This] means that action is always implicitly plural and reciprocal, even when this is not the case in existing circumstances. We have to foreground and *work* that incommensurability to produce a different future. (n.p.)

Varied iterations of such concerns *have* been the focus of numerous critical qualitative education researchers (see, among others, Steinberg & Cannella, 2012; Cannella, Perez, & Pasque, 2015; Denzin & Giardina, 2015, 2016) who have grappled with ethical conundrums generated even prior to, but most certainly since cultural anthropologists George Marcus and Michael Fischer's (1986) calling out the "crisis in representation." For years now, many of us have interrogated not only who gets to appear as "subjects" (and why?) in and of our research, but also "who gets to speak? whose "story" gets told, how, and by whom? and the ever-present "dangers of speaking for others." And multiple indigenous and disabilities studies, for example, have importantly and enormously complicated such issues that permeate all researching attempts, even as we work incessantly toward nonimpositional, nonhierarchical, noncolonizing, nonessentializing assumptions, concepts, and practices.

Many critical qualitative researchers too acknowledge our indebtedness to feminist theorist Donna Haraway's (1988) concept of "situated knowledges" that directly calls into question any positionings of research as neutral and value-free and of its participants as directly observable and able to be fully "knowing" and "known." Haraway's critique includes her interrogating of what she calls "the godtrick"—that assumption of objectivity and thus "a vision that is from everywhere and nowhere" (p. 584) that characterizes positivist research stances. Instead, critical qualitative researchers approach our inquiries knowing that these always will be punctuated by partialities, incoherences, indeterminacies. As part of any reshapings of resistance positionings, we may remind ourselves then of Haraway's exhortation to make productive use of disjointed situations and subjectivities as aspects of a political strategy.

Along these same lines, many of us have attempted what Wanda Pillow (2003) theorizes as "self-reflexivities of discomfort" that challenge us to let the "unfamiliar" remain unfamiliar, to refuse reductions of multiplicities into single and unitary assumptions. Such stances demand that we "interrogate reflexivity's complicit relationship with ethnocentric power and knowledge in qualitative research," including complicit assumptions of the autonomous and fully-knowing "self" that Pillow so abundantly critiques. These kinds of interrogations, similar to all to which I have gestured throughout here, push "toward an unfamiliar, towards the uncomfortable, ... as practices of confounding disruptions" (p. 192) at every turn in our researching.

Such confoundings are aspects of always contingent and constant refashionings, experimentings that I obviously support as necessary aspects of a critical qualitative research that daily entangles with myriad tensions, challenges, and even threats now pervading our researching and teaching endeavors. I've thus quickly skimmed a few generative critiquings and possible reconfigurings of any essentialized notions of "the woman card" dealt to Hillary by a disembodied hand, for example, as one miniature effort toward such work. And I continue working toward reshapings of potential resistance positionings that point to critique *as always immanent* action that, albeit caught up in the very processes, discourses, and materialities in which it is entangled, might aid in learning to think differently about ourselves, even as we strive to always remember that critics need to acknowledge and be scrupulously vigilant (hyper-self-reflexive) in relation to our complicities (Spivak, 1988); historical analysis of the limits that are imposed on us that encourage experiments with the possibility of going beyond these limits; necessities of heightened curiosity and accompanying experimentations in the very conceptualizings and becomings of existence.

Incessant challengings ...

I yell at the television screen highlighting the latest daily Twitter storm; I mutter my mantra back to the screen: I *will* persist in reshapings, reconfigurings of "woman"—and of any other unitary representation of "identity" that leads to stereotyping or excluding or denigrating or acts of violence against any deemed "less than." I *will* daily work on my conjurings of a deck of cards that *refuses* to deal out historically reified and degenerative "meanings." I *will* continue to imagine—on the subway, in the corner bodega, through halls of the institution in which I teach—a deck that instead deals uncomfortable, unfamiliar complexities, one that scatters multiplicities of subjectivities as well as constant reshapings of critical resistance research efforts.

Try playing THAT deck and its a-signifying cards, Donald Trump!

References

Alexander, M. (2010). *The new Jim Crow: Mass incarceration in the age of colorblindness.* New York, NY: The New Press.

Atwood, M. (2017, April 26). Commentary. *USA Today*, p. 3D.

Barad, K. (2007). *Meeting the universe halfway: Quantum physics and the entanglement of matter and meaning.* Durham, NC: Duke University Press.

Blake, J. (2012, November 12). Parallels to country's racist past haunt age of Obama. *CNN.com.* http://inamerica.blogs.cnn.com/2012/11/01/parallels-to-countrys-racist-past-haunt-age-of-obama/

Blake, J. (2016, November 19). "This is what "whitelash" looks like." *CNN.com.* https://www.cnn.com/2016/11/11/us/obama-trump-white-backlash/

Bordo, S. (2017a). *The destruction of Hillary Clinton.* Brooklyn, NY: Melville House Publishing.

Bordo, S. (2017b, June 22). "Why won't she behave?" The demand for Hillary Clinton to apologize. *Medium.* https://medium.com/@susanbordo/why-wont-she-behave-the-demand-for-hillary-clinton-to-apologize-2235d28b8ef

Braidotti, R. (2018). A theoretical framework for critical posthumanities. *Theory, Culture, Society,* 0(0), 1–31. doi:10.1177/0263276418771486

Braidotti, R., & Hlavajova, M. (Eds.). (2018). *Posthuman glossary.* London, England: Bloomsbury Academic.

Butler, J. (1990). *Gender trouble: Feminism and the subversion of identity.* London, England: Routledge.

Butler, J. (1992). Contingent foundations: Feminism and the question of "post-modernism." In J. Butler & J.W. Scott (Eds.), *Feminists theorize the political* (pp. 3–21). New York, NY: Routledge.
Butler, J. (1997). *The psychic life of power.* Stanford, CA: Stanford University Press.
Butler, J. (2004a). *Precarious life: The power of mourning and violence.* New York, NY: Verso.
Butler, J. (2004b). *Undoing gender.* London, England: Routledge.
Butler, J. (2009). *Frames of war: When is life grievable?* New York, NY: Verso.
Butler, J. (2015a). *Notes toward a performative theory of assembly.* Cambridge, MA: Harvard University Press.
Butler, J. (2015b). *Senses of the subject.* New York, NY: Fordham University Press.
Butler, J. (2017, January 18). Reflections on Trump. [Online forum post.] https://culanth.org/fieldsights/1032-reflections-on-trump
Butler, J., & Athanasiou, A. (2013). *Dispossession: The performative in the political.* Cambridge, England: Polity Press.
Butler, J., & Berbee, S. (2017, June 26). We are worldless without one another: An interview with Judith Butler. *The Other Journal: An Intersection of Theology and Culture.* Retrieved from https://theotherjournal.com/2017/06/26/worldless-without-one-another-interview-judith-butler/
Cannella, G.S. (1997). *Deconstructing early childhood education: Social justice and revolution.* New York, NY: Peter Lang.
Cannella, G.S., Perez, M.S., & Pasque, P.A. (Eds). (2015). *Critical qualitative inquiry: Foundations and futures.* Walnut Creek, CA: Left Coast Press.
Cannella, G.S., & Lincoln, Y.S. (2015). Deploying qualitative methods for critical social purposes. In G. Cannella, M.S. Perez, & P.A. Dasque (Eds.), *Critical qualitative inquiry: Foundations and futures* (pp. 243–263). Walnut Creek, CA: Left Coast Press.
Chaillan, P. (2018, April 2). Thinking in alliance: An interview with Judith Butler. Retrieved from https://www.versobooks.com/blogs/3718-thinking-in-alliance-an-interview-with-judith-butler.
Childers, S.M. (2017). Commentary on the Women's March on Washington: How does one become one million? *Educational Studies, 53*(3), 315–318.
Choice, The. (2016, October 31). *The New Yorker,* pp. 31–35.
Clinton, H.R. (2017). *What happened.* New York, NY: Simon & Schuster.
Crenshaw, K. (1989). Demarginalizing the intersection of race and sex: A Black feminist critique of antidiscrimination doctrine, feminist theory, and antiracist politics. *University of Chicago Legal Forum* (pp. 138–167). Chicago, IL: University of Chicago Press.
Davies, B. (1993). *Shards of glass: Children reading and writing beyond gendered identities.* Sydney, Australia: Allen & Unwin.
Davies, B. (2000). *A body of writing.* Lanham, MD: AltaMira Press.
Denzin, N.K. (1997). *Interpretive ethnography: Ethnographic practice for the 21st century.* Thousand Oaks, CA: SAGE.

Denzin, N.K., & Giardina, M.D. (Eds.). (2015). *Qualitative inquiry—past, present, future: A critical reader.* Walnut Creek, CA: Left Coast Press.

Denzin, N.K., & Giardina, M.D. (Eds.). (2016). *Qualitative inquiry through a critical lens.* New York, NY: Routledge.

Denzin, N.K., & Lincoln, Y.S. (2000). *The handbook of qualitative research* (2nd ed.). Thousand Oaks, CA: SAGE.

Eisenstein, Z. (2016). Hillary Clinton's imperial feminism. *Cairo Review, 23,* 50–56.

Foucault, M. (1984). What is enlightenment? C. Porter, trans. In P. Rabinow (Ed.), *The Foucault reader* (pp. 32–50). New York, NY: Pantheon Books.

Foucault, M. (1988). *Michel Foucault: Politics, philosophy, culture.* L.D. Kritzman, ed.; A. Sheridan et al., trans. New York, NY: Routledge.

Gilmore, L. (2012). Agency without mastery: Chronic pain and posthuman life writing. *Biography, 35*(1), 83–98.

Grant, J. (2018). A left feminist comment on supporting Hillary Clinton. *Politics and Gender,* 14:1. doi:10.1017/S1743923X17000563

Guba, E.G. (1990). The alternative paradigm dialog. In E.G. Guba (Ed.), *The paradigm dialog* (pp. 17–30). Newbury Park, CA: SAGE.

Guba, E.G., & Lincoln, Y.S. (2005). Paradigmatic controversies and emerging confluences. In N. K. Denzin & Y. S. Lincoln (Eds.), *Handbook of qualitative research* (3rd ed., pp. 191–216). Thousand Oaks, CA: SAGE.

Hammersley, M. (2008). *Questioning qualitative inquiry: Critical essays.* Thousand Oaks, CA: SAGE.

Haraway, D. (1988). Situated knowledges: The science question in feminism and the privilege of partial perspective. *Feminist Studies, 14,* 575–599.

Haraway, D. (1991). *Simians, cyborgs, and women: The reinvention of nature.* New York, NY: Routledge.

Hekman, S. (2014). *The feminine subject.* Cambridge, England: Polity Press.

hooks, b. (1992). *Black looks: Race and representation.* Toronto, Canada: Between the Lines Press.

Lather, P. (1991). *Getting smart: Feminist research and pedagogy with/in the postmodern.* New York, NY: Routledge.

Lather, P. (1993). Fertile obsession: Validity after poststructuralism. *The Sociological Quarterly, 34*(4), 673–693.

Lather, P. (1995). Post-critical pedagogies: A feminist reading. In P. McLaren (Ed.), *Postmodernism, post-colonialism and pedagogy* (pp. 167–186). Albert Park, Australia: James Nicholas.

Lather, P. (2016). Top 10+ List: (Re)thinking ontology in post qualitative research. *Critical Studies <=> Critical Methodologies, 16*(2), 125–131.

Lather, P. (2017). Dear Hillary. *International Journal of Qualitative Studies in Education, 30*(10), 971–974. doi:10.1080/09518398.2017.1312601

Lather, P., & St. Pierre, E.A. (2013). Post qualitative research. *International Journal of Qualitative Studies in Education, 26*, 629–633.

Lincoln, Y.S. (1998). From understanding to action: New imperatives, new criteria, new methods for interpretive researchers. *Theory and Research in Social Education, 26*(1), 12–29.

Lorde, A. (1984). *Sister outsider.* Trumansburg, NY: The Crossing Press.

MacClure, M. (2013). Researching without representation? Language and materiality in post qualitative methodology. *International Journal of Qualitative Studies in Education, 26*(6), 658–667.

MacClure, M. (2015). The new materialisms: A thorn in the flesh of critical qualitative inquiry? In G. Cannella, M. S. Perez, & P. A. Dasque (Eds.), *Critical qualitative inquiry: Foundations and futures* (pp. 93–112). Walnut Creek, CA: Left Coast Press.

Marcus, G.E., & Fischer, M.M.J. (1986). *Writing as cultural critique: An experimental moment in the human sciences.* Chicago, IL: University of Chicago Press.

Mead, R. (2017, April 17). The prophet of dystopia: Margaret Atwood's dark "speculative fiction" eerily anticipates today's crisis. *The New Yorker,* pp. 38–47.

Miller, J.L. (1990). *Creating spaces and finding voices: Teachers collaborating for empowerment.* Albany, NY: State University of New York Press.

Miller, J.L. (2005). *Sounds of silence breaking: Women, curriculum, autobiography.* New York, NY: Peter Lang.

Miller, J.L. (2017). Neo-positivist intrusions, post-qualitative challenges, and PAR'S generative indeterminacies. *International Journal of Qualitative Studies in Education, 30*(5), 488–503. doi:10.1080/09518398.2017.1303215

Newton-Small, J. (2016, February 8). Madeleine Albright defends her Hillary Clinton remarks. *Time Magazine.com.* http://time.com/4212577/madeleine-albright-hillary-clinton-special-place-hell-defends/

Pillow, W.S. (2003). Confession, catharsis, or cure: The use of reflexivity as methodological power in qualitative research. *International Journal of Qualitative Studies in Education, 16*(2), 175–196.

Pillow, W.S. (2018, April 15). Discussant comments. Paper presented in symposium Surviving and Countering Patriarchal Whitelash: Public Education and Resistance Research, Annual Conference of the American Educational Research Association, New York, NY.

Remnick, D. (2017, November 20). Autumn of the patriarchy. *The New Yorker,* pp. 31–32.

Smith, S. (2012). Reading the posthuman backward: Mary Rowlandson's double witnessing. *Biography, 35*(1), 137–152.

Spivak, G.C. (1988). *In other worlds: Essays in cultural politics.* London, England: Routledge.

Spivak, G.C., & Arteaga, A. (1995). Bonding in difference. In D. Landry & G. MacLean (Eds.), *The Spivak reader,* (pp. 15–28). New York, NY: Routledge.

Steinberg, S., & Cannella, G.S. (Eds.). (2012). *Critical qualitative research reader.* New York, NY: Peter Lang.

St. Pierre, E.A. (2011). Post qualitative research: The critique and the coming after. In N.K. Denzin & Y.S. Lincoln (Eds.), *The SAGE handbook of qualitative research* (pp. 611–625). Thousand Oaks, CA: SAGE.

St. Pierre, E.A. (2013). The posts continue: Becoming. *International Journal of Qualitative Studies in Education, 26*, 646–657.

St. Pierre, E.A. (2014). A brief and personal history of post qualitative research: Toward "post" inquiry. *JCT: Journal of Curriculum Theorizing, 30*(2), 2–19.

St. Pierre, E.A., Jackson, A., & Mazzei, L.A. (2016). New empiricisms and new materialisms. *Cultural Studies <=> Critical Methodologies, 16*, 99–110.

St. Pierre, E. & Pillow, W.S. (2000). (Eds.). *Working the ruins: Feminist poststructural theory and methods in education.* New York, NY: Routledge.

Taguchi, H.L. (2013). Images of thinking in feminist materialisms: Ontological divergences and the production of research subjectivities. *International Journal of Qualitative Studies in Education, 26*(6), 706–716.

Tamboukou, M. (2008). A Foucauldian approach to narratives. In M. Andrews, C. Squire, & M. Tamboukou (Eds.), *Doing narrative research* (1st ed., pp. 88–107). London, England: SAGE.

CHAPTER SIX

Resisting Patriarchy
Explorations Using a Collaborative Protest Play

Gaile S. Cannella

THE CONTENT AND activities included in this protest play were created as reactions to the campaigns and defeat of Hillary Clinton by Donald Trump in the U.S. presidential election of 2016, along with the subsequent actions of Trump over the first year of his administration. The play was created in an attempt to conduct critical research that would be shared in ways that could leave the audience with a more affirmative resistance reaction to a very difficult, unjust situation, as well as ideas for future public action. Versions of the play were used as the final activities following two traditional research paper presentations. The reader will note that the play involves the entire audience both speaking as a group and as assigned to individual roles. Further, all take part in the first aid and collaborative puzzle activities.

As historical research, the voices and work of many from the past are entangled with contemporary actors. At times these voices are directly quoted; at other times, they are paraphrased or grouped together. From within this perspective, the purpose of the play is to begin the exploration of the following: (a) how we make present the historical scholarship, voices, actions, struggles, and diverse lives of those who have come before, as well as how we "becomewith" (Haraway, 2015, p. 11) all manner of diversity; and (b) action possibilities for using traditional marginalized and emergent perspectives that acknowledge human becomingswith each other and the more than human in ways that challenge sexism, racism, and other forms of injustice that continue to harm and destroy.

While the particular events tied to the new presidency were the immediate motivation, the reader-participant is reminded that the focus of the performance is played out every day in the lives of so many women of all colors and persuasions in the United States, as well as around the globe. The contemporary and related historical investigations are used to explore public performance possibilities that can unveil misogyny and intersectional oppression along with enabling participants to collaboratively becomewith persistent, nonviolent resistance and forms of affirmative survival.

****

RESISTING and COUNTERING PATRIARCHY: A PLAY IN TWO ACTS

The director or host is encouraged to make changes or revisions as fits the circumstances. Examples are: add more quotes and/or posters; darken lights between scenes. Further, the intermission and finale activities may be revised—for example, action projects laid out on puzzles rather than sayings for signs. Before beginning the play (possibly even before papers in a more traditional session), assign the roles.

Roles to Be Cast

    Host (who will explain all activities; usually the organizer of the play)

    Narrators One (migrant woman), Two (woman of color), Three (white woman)

    Play booklet to all Audience participants so all can read the audience narrative

    Three Poster leaders

    Persistent roles that include

        Navajo woman

        Punjabi man

        Elder Marie Jones

Three audience members who will together represent Intersectional Injustice

Three audience members who will together represent Power Complexities

Five audience members who will together represent Voices of Indigenous Peoples

Canadian First Nations Individual

Postcolonial Scholar

Mitch McConnell

Rosa Parks

Winona LaDuke

Lavern Cox

Ruby Bridges

Lilly Ledbetter

Malala Yousafzai

Susan B. Anthony

Angela Davis

Sylvia Rivera

Ilhan Omar

ACT I
The Misogynous Condition: Understanding Misogyny, Intersectional Hate, Uninformed Reinscriptions

HOST: Scene 1, recognizing and acknowledging misogyny

NARRATOR ONE: "At the 2016 Republican National Convention (*for the presidency*) in the United States, a fervent hostility was hard to miss (*regarding the*

democrat, female candidate). Inside the hall, delegates repeatedly broke into chants of 'Lock her up'." Outside the hall, vendors sold campaign paraphernalia like:

> A pin reading, DON'T BE A PUSSY, VOTE FOR TRUMP
>
> Another pin reading, FINALLY SOMEONE WITH BALLS
>
> A t-shirt reading, HILLARY SUCKS BUT NOT LIKE MONICA
>
> Another pin reading, LIFE'S A BITCH, DON'T VOTE FOR ONE
>
> Another pin reading, KFC HILLARY SPECIAL, TWO FAT THIGHS, TWO SMALL BREASTS – LEFT WING (quote from Beinart, 2016)

AUDIENCE: "Mysogyny is the law enforcement branch of patriarchy" (Manne, interviewed by Illing, 2018).

NARRATOR TWO: Not surprising to most women, when Hillary Clinton fulfilled traditionally identified roles that were expected of her as a woman—roles like serving as a loyal secretary of state to Obama, standing by her husband when he was in trouble, and functioning like a traditional first lady who always/already stands for women's issues—she tended to be popular. However, when she violated those roles—like heading a health care task force or running for president—she was much less popular. (Beinart, 2016).

AUDIENCE: "Mysogyny is the law enforcement branch of patriarchy." (Manne, interviewed by Illing, 2018).

NARRATOR THREE: According to a range of studies, at least some men tend to fear emasculation. Subordination to women seems to bring on this fear for many. Some women even tend to be threatened by challenges to traditional gender roles. Why is this relevant to a female candidate for the U.S presidency? Or to a female CEO? Or to a female dean? According to Beinart (2016) it is because people who "dislike[d] Hillary Clinton for president most are those who most fear emasculation." This fear influences judgment related to women in any supervisory role.

NARRATOR ONE: Further, others (who may even have voted for her) have perpetuated the nasty woman view, as Trump referred to Clinton in the debates—and have even accepted the discourse that she is likely dishonest, even if *not as bad as "Trump."* Even many of her supporters have demonstrated the continued acceptance of woman as questionable, dishonest, sneaky, not quite good enough (just slightly better than the more "evil" other). How many of us as women can identify with this attitude and the behavior that we have experienced associated with it? Whatever we do is not kind enough, not smart enough, not tough enough, is too calculated or too self-interested—ESPECIALLY IF IT SUBORDINATES MALES IN ANY WAY—or, if a guy feels subordinated.

AUDIENCE: "Mysogyny is the law enforcement branch of patriarchy" (Manne, interviewed by Illing, 2018).

NARRATOR TWO: So, how do we understand misogyny?

NARRATOR THREE: Misogyny is not the hatred of all women, which is a naïve conception with serious limitations. Misogyny would not attempt to "rid the world of women" ... women are, in fact, "thoroughly integrated into prototypical patriarchal households ... such women are too useful to the dominant ..." (Manne, 2017, p. 53). Rather, "misogyny might be understood as the system that operates within a patriarchal social order to police and enforce women's subordination and to uphold male dominance" (p. 33).

AUDIENCE: "Mysogyny is the law enforcement branch of patriarchy" (Manne, interviewed by Illing, 2018).

NARRATOR ONE: "Misogynists can love their mothers—not to mention their sisters, daughters, wives, girlfriends, and secretaries. They need not hate women universally, or even very generally. They tend to hate women who are outspoken, among other things" (Manne, 2017, p. 52).

NARRATOR TWO: "The victims of misogyny hence tend to be women entering positions of power and authority over men, and women eschewing or opting out of male-oriented service roles. Among others, its natural targets will be (surprise) feminists" (Manne, 2017, p. 51).

AUDIENCE: "Mysogyny is the law enforcement branch of patriarchy" (Manne, interviewed by Illing, 2018).

NARRATOR THREE: "This misogyny is global, with Russia as an example. The move to partially 'decriminalize' domestic violence in Russia in January, 2017, is the illustrative apex of a longer trajectory of the decimation of women's rights post-Pussy Riot .... It is evident that the local neoconservative context in Russia is hardening. We are seeing legislation limiting women's autonomy and freedom by attacking reproductive rights and disregarding gender-based violence... it is important to consider these moves as situated within a global context of apparent state-sanctioned misogynies" (Turbine, 2017).

AUDIENCE: "Mysogyny is the law enforcement branch of patriarchy" (Manne, interviewed by Illing, 2018).

NARRATOR THREE: "In the movie *Trumpland*, Michael Moore demonstrates how Trump is seen as the great white hope for many white men, as the last chance to restore a luster to the dominant, patriarchal brand of masculinity. After viewing the movie with an audience in Ohio, Moore tells the audience that Trump projects the business image of a rough and tumble 'man's man' and the caring Big Daddy. Moore further imitates the White male supporters at Trump rallies, growling like 'dying dinosaurs.' [Moore] says to them, 'We had a good run at being in charge guys—10,000 years. It's women's turn'" (Okun, 2016).

POSTERS *(poster leaders stand and present and further suggest audience repetition, however the action fits the circumstances)*:

   I Shall Not Change My Course Because Those Who Assume to Be Better than I Desire It (Victoria Woodhull, 1st female candidate for U.S. president, 1872)

   I have a brain and a uterus and I use both (Patricia Shroeder, Former U.S. Representative)

   Both Putin and Trump Aren't Just Anti-Feminist. They Demean Women (Nadya Tolokonnikova, [2017] member of Pussy Riot)

HOST: Scene 2, Intersectional Feminisms and Complexity

HOST: We can't even begin to address misogyny without engaging with intersecting identities, life experiences, bodies, and inequities—and TRUMP CERTAINLY MADE HATE INTERSECTIONAL. **WE NEED INTERSECTIONAL FEMINISMS!!**

NARRATOR ONE: Because of our complex lives, we can think of intersectionality as meaning "paying attention to the ways the gender-based discrimination and oppression a woman may experience can be compounded by her race, socioeconomic status, sexual orientation, and more" (Desmond-Harris, 2017).

NARRATOR TWO: "*Misogynoir* is Moya Bailey's term for the potent intersection of anti-Black racism and misogyny faced by African American women in the U.S." ... White women can "easily be made complicit in not only misogyny in general, but misogynoir in particular ... We need more voices on the subject. And I think the same applies to trans misogyny, too. We need more trans voices urgently" (Manne, quoted in Penaluna, 2018).

AUDIENCE: We need intersectional feminisms and transformative actions!!!!

NARRATOR THREE: "Women's rights" organizers *(of the Women's March around the globe following the U.S. 2016 presidential campaign)* took care to make it clear that they mean ALL women of ALL backgrounds ... focusing on not only suffragists and abolitionists, but the Civil Rights movement, the American Indian movement, and Black Lives Matter—even while facing criticism from the left and the right. The organizers note: "Women have intersecting identities and are therefore impacted by a multitude of social justice and human rights issues." Examples include the especially urgent need for equal pay among Women of Color and the way they're uniquely victimized by the criminal justice system (Desmond-Harris, 2017).

NARRATOR ONE: Although President Barack Obama's election (and successes) would lead many to believe that white racism against People of Color had been eliminated, this does not seem to be the case. Several research studies since 2011 have indicated that the Obama presidency seems to have given some some who identify as white "the perceived moral license to express more critical attitudes about minorities" (Beinart, 2016). Further, this emboldened racism seems to have interacted with misogynous forms of policing as a woman ran for the presidency

AUDIENCE: We need intersectional feminisms and transformative actions!!!!

NARRATOR TWO: "The story of the United States for many is a never-ending process of playing catch-up. The perspective of those at the back of the line has been a tunnel-vision reality of knowing who is holding you down. Black people focus on white racists, gay people are consumed with protecting themselves from homophobes, women struggle to exist freely in a man's world, Muslims and Mexican immigrants feel the weight of the world against them from *(self-identified)* "true" Americans. This created a complicated ecosystem for the historically abused—a shared understanding of what it means to be discriminated against, but also a quiet resentment over who has it worse.... Now we're faced with a clear reality—one group that hates us all" (Browne, 2016).

AUDIENCE: We need intersectional feminisms and transformative actions!!!!

NARRATOR THREE: "So many men hate the idea of capable women breaking into all-male spaces, because with her comes instant accountability ... YEAH, IT'S HATE ... but white supremacy and patriarchy have always also been based in fear. Trump's election is a sign that every other group in this country was getting too smart—too skilled—too American—too fast" (Browne, 2016).

AUDIENCE: We need intersectional feminisms and transformative actions!!!!

POSTERS:

> I am not free while any woman is unfree, even when her shackles are very different than my own (Lorde, 1984).

> The women who sustained me were black and white, old and young, lesbian, bisexual, and heterosexual, and we all shared a war against the tyrannies of silence (Lorde, 1984).

HOST: Scene 3: Recognizing and Avoiding Reinscriptions

NARRATOR ONE: "Women are used to men weighing in on issues pertaining to us, a behavior that many have come to call mansplaining. Nothing seems to be off limits for discussion. Nothing—not our rights, our bodies, our choices of clothing, how we talk, or even our thoughts. This is not new. In fact, we've come to expect it. It often feels like we can never have a conversation about our lived experience without some guy who thinks he knows better than we do" (Macias, 2017).

NARRATOR TWO: David Brooks is an excellent example of a mansplainer as he "enlightens" all of us lowly women about the Women's March. He gets it wrong, but that doesn't stop him from thinking he can explain how the "world" works to all of us. Here's an example from one of his articles:

> [P]rogressives seem intent on doubling down on exactly what has doomed them so often ... identity politics isolates progressives ... fixation on diversity produced a generation of liberals and progressives

narcissistically unaware of conditions outside their self-defined groups ... further, the central threat is not the patriarchy ... (Brooks, in Macias, 2017).

NARRATOR THREE: "There goes the mansplaining again, telling women that patriarchy is not the problem. Funny how when women, People of Color, immigrants, Muslims, and others who are not in the mainstream expand the conversation to include our issues, it gets labeled as 'identity politics' and 'divisive.' To make it crystal clear, patriarchy is a huge problem. Patriarchy and racism intersect, are reasons for wage gaps, and the unacknowledged rape culture" (Macias, 2017).

POSTERS:

I Will Not Go Quietly Back to the 1950s

The Election of Trump Will Be Recorded as Patriarchy's Last Stand

The master's tools will never dismantle the master's house (Lorde, 1984)

INTERMISSION: *"Fighting Misogyny Survival Kit" (may also be labeled "Fighting Oppression First Aid Kit"). HOST explains gift that is distributed to each audience member. Participants may explore their kits and talk about them during the 10–15 minute intermission. See the end of the play for content.*

ACT II
Challenging the Patriarchal Capitalocene

HOST: Scene 1: Make present and becomewith those who have come before

NARRATOR ONE: There are no limits to our possibilities if we consider those who have come before—if we consider their lives, knowledges, actions, and treatment by those who have dominated. As scholars, researchers, and educators, we are in the unique position that requires the historical awareness of diverse knowledges and lifeways as well as forms of scholarship that unveil and support all manner of diversity.

NARRATOR TWO: Multiple academic volumes and life stories have provided us with all types of possibilities and information. Yet, we have not usually becomewith these multiples. Making present and becomingwith requires knowing about, researching, listening, hearing, reading—and a willingness to engage openly and respectfully—and to becomewith diverse her/histories and multiplicities.

AUDIENCE: We protest in support of multiplicities and those who have come before.

NAVAJO WOMAN: "I am also a warrior person as specified by my Diné name *(a label that you might call Navajo)*. I am not a warrior "princess." ... Oral histories of Hweeldi/The Long Walk provide examples of Diné women who courageously led or supported their people to survival" (Cannella & Manuelito, 2008, p. 55).

PUNJABI MAN: "I come from a land and peoples for whom the White, home-churned butter is deemed divine—the food stolen by their beloved god-child, Krishna.... My people are indigenous to the Punjab.... The Punjabis, like all other indigenous peoples, have learned to adjust to every aspect of their bioregions: including the blistering hot *loo* (the summer wind ... that soars heat into the 140s ...). In millions of homes ... *lassi* (a sweet and salty summer yoghurt drink) is served to cool people down ... [and is even referred to as] 'the air-conditioner of the Punjab'" (Prakash, 1999, p. 173).

ELDER MARY JONES, Short Hills Harvest, 2016: If you listen to the four legged they will teach you (Legge & Taha, 2017, p. 63).

AUDIENCE: We protest in support of multiplicities and those who have come before.

NARRATOR THREE: Perhaps critical research and critical education are not possible without recognizing that justice for all human groups, the environment, and for other-than-human animals is not possible without acknowledging the intersectionality of all forms of injustice. While we have acknowledged intersectionality, do we always function as if we understand the complexities and the ways that some attempts to increase specific forms of justice actually foster injustice broadly? And, do we support "others" as they attempt to survive these oppressive complexities?

NARRATOR ONE: Along with the years and years of diverse her/his(s)tories that have most often been silenced—those of indigenous groups, People of Color, and women (just to name a view)—some forms of contemporary research and education also acknowledge human privilege (however White and male the character).

NARRATOR TWO: Therefore, researchers and educators increasingly inhabit spaces in which the oppressive intersectionalities that are more-than-human cannot be ignored. These acknowledgements generate different languages, unthought concepts, and potentially new forms of action. Further, the more broad based the understanding, perhaps the greater the possibilities for the elimination of systemic domination, violence, and intersecting oppression—for literally rethinking, reconceptualizing, and transforming.

AUDIENCE: We protest for the always/already recognition of oppressive intersectionalities, power complexities, and possibilities for change.

THREE AUDIENCE MEMBERS as Intersectional Justice: We represent intersectional justice. "For most of U.S. history, most efforts to protect the environment were actually only meant to preserve it for a select few. And that often meant deliberately placing pollutants in the neighborhoods of marginalized Americans" (quoted from Ahmed, 2018).

THREE AUDIENCE MEMBERS as the Complexities of Power: We are the complexities of power. "The discursive tie between the colonized, the enslaved, the noncitizen, and the animal—all reduced to type, all Others to rational man, and all essential to his bright constitution—is at the heart of racism and flourishes, lethally, in the entrails of humanism" (Haraway, 2008, p. 18).

FIVE AUDIENCE MEMBERS as voices of Indigenous Peoples: We are some of the voices of the many indigenous peoples. The multiplicities of engagement with other beings of the world are dialogues considered of utmost importance. As Andeans we believe that "Dialogue does not lead one to a knowledge about the other but rather to attune oneself to its mode of being, and in company with that other, to generate and regenerate life" (Apffel-Marglin, 1995, p. 13, in Prakash, 1999, p. 170).

THREE AUDIENCE MEMBERS as the Complexities of Power: "Feminism, antiracist, and postcolonial studies on the one hand and posthumanism on the other must supplement each other" (Snaza, 2013, p. 48).

NARRATOR THREE: Just as becomingswith implies unthought ways of being and thinking, and not a dualistic becoming Other, becomingswith occur in unanticipated contact zones between/with critical histories, indigenous knowledges, and views that challenge human privilege. New connections, beings, and bodies become new possibilities for change—through/with hybrid embodiments, multi-sensorial languages, multispecicies relations, and symbiotic entanglements.

HOST: Scene 2: Thinking/Researching/Acting

NARRATOR ONE: When we choose to act, reconceptualizations are an absolute necessity, especially within current misogynous, neoliberal, and troubled political conditions. Reconceptualization involves resistance through respect and rethinking research goals and purposes.

ENTIRE GROUP: Value and respect, build coalitions, resist, persist, take action, and report these actions through research.

Canadian First Nations Woman: "The real justification for including Aboriginal knowledge in the modern curriculum is not so that Aboriginal students can compete with non-Aboriginal students in an imagined world. It is, rather, that immigrant society (all non-Aboriginal peoples) is sorely in need of what Aboriginal knowledge has to offer" (Battiste, 2000, p. 201).

Postcolonial Scholar: "A transnational feminist practice depends on building feminist solidarities across the divisions of place, identity, class, work, belief.... In these very fragmented times it is both very difficult to build these alliances and also never more important to do so" (Mohanty, 2003, p. 250).

ENTIRE GROUP: Value and respect, build coalitions, resist, persist, take action, and report these actions through research.

NARRATOR ONE: We have so many examples of our sisters who **RESIST, ACT, and PERSIST**:

NARRATOR THREE: The imagery of a man silencing a woman is all too common to most of us. Mitch McConnell and other Republicans performed the attempted silencing on Senator Elizabeth Warren. "As Jeff Sessions was being considered for Attorney General in early 2017, Senator Warren was trying to read a letter written in 1986 by Coretta Scott King regarding her concerns about racism exhibited by Mr. Sessions as he was considered for a judgeship. Senator Warren was accused of violating a rule that forbids demeaning another senator and was interrupted before reading Mrs. King's statement" (McCann, 2017).

NARRATOR ONE: The King letter and detailed statement (already on the Congressional record from 1986) criticized Mr. Sessions for using "the awesome power of his office to chill the free exercise of the vote by Black citizens" while serving as a United States attorney in Alabama (King, quoted in McCann, 2017).

NARRATOR TWO: "Although Senator Warren attempted to explain that this is an appropriate document for a confirmation hearing, Mitch McConnell firmly dismissed her—later saying:

> SHE WAS WARNED. SHE WAS GIVEN AN EXPLANATION. NEVERTHELESS, SHE PERSISTED. Further, she was told: THE SENATOR WILL TAKE HER SEAT (Victor, 2017).

NARRATOR THREE: In the end, Senator Warren had her say. She read the statement from Mrs. King in full on Facebook. Further, this became a battle cry for all of us, as Hillary Clinton posted on February 8, 2017:

> "She was warned. She was given an explanation.
>
> Nevertheless, she persisted."
>
> So must we all. —Hillary Clinton (@HillaryClinton) (Victor, 2017)

ENTIRE GROUP: We have so many examples of our sisters who **PERSIST. SHE WAS WARNED. NEVERTHELESS, SHE PERSISTED!!!**

Each activist should stand as she speaks (and remain standing).

Ilhan Omar: My name is Ilhan Omar. I am a Somali-American former refugee. I was recently elected to the U.S. House of Representatives.

Rosa Parks: My name is Rosa Parks. I am a black woman who refused to give up my seat to a white passenger on the bus. I believed this to be important for civil rights.

Winona LaDuke: My name is Winona LaDuke. I fight for environmental justice locally and globally.

AUDIENCE: NEVERTHELESS, SHE PERSISTED!!!

Laverne Cox: My name is Laverne Cox. I am an advocate for the trans community.

Ruby Bridges: Facing a protesting white mob, I became the first black child in an all-white school. My name is Ruby Bridges.

Lilly Ledbetter: I sued my employer to champion equal rights for women. I am Lilly Ledbetter.

AUDIENCE: NEVERTHELESS, SHE PERSISTED!!!

Malala Yousafzai: My name is Malala Yousafzai. Even after being "shot in the head," I know I must continue to speak out for girls' rights.

Susan B. Anthony: My name is Susan Anthony. In 1872, I was arrested as an abolitionist and suffragette.

Angela Davis: I am Angela Davis. Equal rights are of major importance to me, even when faced with "trumped up" crimes.

Sylvia Rivera: I am Sylvia Rivera. I must be a voice in the LBGTQ Liberation movement.

AUDIENCE: NEVERTHELESS, SHE PERSISTED!!!

HOST: In these difficult times, what do we do? "We are entangled as researchers, even if some interconnections appear closer than others" (Ulmer, 2017, p. 848). So, we acknowledge and work with our entanglements.

ENTIRE GROUP: We push for science that is by the people (Prakash, 1999). We "re-member"—pushing past the intended divisions of patriarchy, colonialism, and capitalism, revisioning our research toward justice (Grande & McCarty, 2018, p. 166). We persist, act, persist, and act again.

AUDIENCE: NEVERTHELESS, SHE PERSISTED!!!

COLLABORATIVE ACTION PUZZLES FINALE

This play finale is a **HOST**-explained collaborative activity. Using the puzzle piece found in the Fighting Misogyny kit, each audience member looks for the other eight audience members with puzzle pieces that will complete the collaborative sign/action. Each group then shares the collaboratively completed puzzle with the larger group.

Explanations of Activities
Fighting Misogyny (or Oppression) Survival Kit

The following items are made and placed into a kit (small plastic container) for each audience member.

(1) A whistle with the note "for when no one is paying attention" (from FEAS);

(2) Fair trade, cruelty free, vegan, organic oils, non-GMO soap with the note "to wash away the stench of intersectional oppression (or patriarchy)";

(3) Small bag labeled "Anti-Depression Supports" that contains pictures of more-than-human companions and chocolates;

(4) Home-crafted charm labeled "This charm can be a necklace or key chain. It stands for the sparkle that you add to the lives of all through your fight to increase justice and end oppression. THANK YOU!"

(5) Puzzle piece that will be used in the final play activity. The HOST directs audience members to save the puzzle piece for the play finale.

Collaborative Action Puzzles

The following are signs placed on nine-piece puzzles, one sign on each puzzle, and taken apart for distribution in survival kits. After the play is completed, each audience member is told to find the other eight people who have puzzle pieces that match hers/his to complete the puzzle and to read the sign.

Respect existence or expect resistance.

Nasty women make (her)story.

Glass ceilings are meant to be broken.

Your laws will destroy the dreams of millions. (Vaglanos & Dahlen, 2017)

A woman's place is in the revolution. (Schulte, 2011)

Revolution is not a one-time event. (Lorde, 1984, p. 140)

Girls just wanna have "fun"damental human rights.

They tried to bury us. They didn't know we were seeds.

Raising our children to tear down your wall (Wickman, 2017).

To all the little girls … never doubt that you are valuable and powerful and deserving of every chance in the world (Clinton, 2016).

References

Ahmed, A. (2018, February 26). We can't truly protect the environment unless we tackle social justice issues, too. *Popular Science*. Retrieved from https://www.popsci.com/environmentalism-inclusive-justice#page-4

Apffel-Marglin, F. (1995). Regeneration in the Andes: The Andean peasants' traditional cosmovision as it is being regenerated today. *Interculture, 28* (1), 126.

Battiste, M. (2000). (Ed.) *Reclaiming indigenous voice and vision*. Vancouver, BC, Canada: UBC Press.

Beinart, P. (2016, October). Fear of a female president. *The Atlantic*. Retrieved from https://www.theatlantic.com/magazine/archive/2016/10/fear-of-a-female-president/497564/

Browne, R. (2016, November 9). How Trump made hate intersectional. *New York Magazine*. Retrieved from http://nymag.com/daily/intelligencer/2016/11/how-trump-made-hate-intersectional.html

Cannella, G.S., & Manuelito, K. (2008). Feminisms from unthought locations: Indigenous worldviews, marginalized feminisms, and revisioning an anticolonial social science. In N.K Denzin, Y.S. Lincoln, & L.T. Smith (Eds). *Handbook of critical and indigenous methodologies* (pp. 45-59) Thousand Oaks, CA: Sage.

Clinton, H.R. (2016). Hillary Clinton's concession speech, full transcript: 2016 presidential election. *Vox*. Retrieved from https://www.vox.com/2016/11/9/13570328/hillary-clinton's-concession-speech-full-transcript-2016-presidential-election

Desmond-Harris, J.D. (2017, January 21). To understand the women's march on Washington, you need to understand intersectional feminism. *Vox*. Retrieved from www.vox.com/identities/2017/1/17/14267766/womens-march-on-washington-inauguration-trump-feminism-intersectionality-race-class

Grande, S., & McCarty, T.L (2018). Indigenous elsewhere: Refusal and re-membering in education research, policy, and praxis. *International Journal of Qualitative Studies in Education, 31*(3), 165–167.

Haraway, D.J., (2015). *Staying with the trouble*. Durham, NC: Duke University Press.

Haraway, D.J., (2008). *When species meet*. Minneapolis: University of Minnesota Press.

Illing, S. (2018, updated February 7). What we get wrong about misogyny. *Vox*. Retrieved from https://www.vox.com/identities/2017/12/5/16705284/me-too-weinstein-misogyny-sexism

Legge, M.M., & Taha, R. (2017). "Fake vegans": Indigenous solidarity and animal liberation activism. *Journal of Indigenous Social Development, 6*(1), 63–81.

Lorde, A. (1984). *Sister outsider*. Trumansburg, NY: The Crossing Press.

Macias, K. (2017, January 24). David Brooks mansplains the Women's March and, of course, gets it wrong. *Daily Kos*. Retrieved from https://www.dailykos.com/stories/2017/1/24/1624448/-David-Brooks-mansplains-the-women's-march-and-of-course-gets-it-wrong

Manne, K. (2017). *Down girl: The logic of mysogyny*. Oxford, England: Oxford University Press.

McCann, E. (2017, February 8). Coretta Scott King's 1986 statement to the Senate about Jeff Sessions. *The New York Times*. Retrieved from https://www.nytimes.com/2017/02/08/us/politics/elizabeth-warren-coretta-scott-king-jeff-sessions.html

Mohanty, C.T. (2003). *Feminism without borders: Decolonizing theory, practicing solidarity*. Durham, NC: Duke University Press.

Okun, R. (2016, November 16). White men who voted for Donald Trump must let go of old ways. *Women's News*. Retrieved from https://womensnews.org/2016/22/white-men-who-voted-for-donald-trump-must-let-go-of-old-ways/

Penaluna, R. (2018, February 7). Kate Manne: The shock collar that is misogyny. *Guernica*. Retrieved from https://www.guernicamag.com/kate-manne-why-misogyny-isnt-really-about-hating-women/

Prakash, M.S. (1999). Indigenous knowledge systems: Ecological literacy through initiation into people's science. In L.M. Samali & J.L. Kincheloe (Eds.), *What is indigenous knowledge?* (pp. 157–178). New York, NY: Falmer Press.

Schulte, E. (2011, March 8). A woman's place is in the revolution. SocialistWorker.org. Retrieved from https://socialistworker.org/2011/03/08/womens-place-in-the-revolution

Snaza, N. (2013). Bewildering education. *Journal of Curriculum & Pedagogy, 10*(1), 38–54.

Tolokonnikova, N. (2017, March 20). Advice from Pussy Riot: How to defy Putin and Trump. *Foreign Policy*. Retrieved from https://foreignpolicy.com/2017/03/20/advice-from-pussy-riot-how-to-defy-putin-and-trump/

Turbine, V. (2017, April 5). Russia: Decimation of women's human rights in the context of global misogyny. *New Eastern Europe*. Retrieved from neweasterneurope.eu/2017/04/05/Russia-decimation-of-womens-rights-in-the-context-of-global-misogyny/

Ulmer, J. B. (2017). Posthumanism as research methodology: Inquiry in the Anthropocene. *International Journal of Qualitative Studies in Education, 30*(9), 832–848.

Vaglanos, A., & Dahlen, D. (2017, January 21). 89 badass feminist signs from the Women's March on Washington. *Huffington Post*. Retrieved from https://www.huffingtonpost.com/entry/89-badass-feminist-signs-from-the-women's-march-on-washington_us_5883ea28e4b070d8cad310ed

Victor, D. (2017, February 8). "Nevertheless, she persisted": How Senate's silencing of Warren became a meme. *The New York Times*. https://www.nytimes.com/2017/02/08/us/politics/elizabeth-warren-republicans-facebook-twitter.html

Wickman, F. (2017, January 21). The best protest signs from the women's march on Washington. *Slate*. Retrieved from www.slate.com/blogs/xx_factor/2017/01/21/the_best_protest_signs_from_the_women's_march_on_washington.htm

Additional Resources:

Collaborations Using Protest Puzzles by Gaile S. Cannella, created in 2017.

Fighting Oppression Survival Kit by Gaile S. Cannella, created in 2017 (some content taken from #FEAS).

#FEAS (Feminist Educators Against Sexism). Emily Gray, Linda Knight, Mindy Blaise. Funded by the Australian Association for Research in Education (AARE). Interventions. (n.d.). Retrieved from https://feministeducatorsagainstsexism.com/projects/

CHAPTER SEVEN

Resources for Becomingswith Activism, Research, and Contemporary Politics

Gaile S. Cannella
Yvonna S. Lincoln

Activism, Nonviolent Resistance, and Public Scholarship

CENTURIES OF SUPPORT for diversity, justice, and equity around the globe are obvious as social movement histories have revealed massive public actions. However, probably the most closely tied movements related to current possibilities for critical qualitative inquiry are Mahatma Gandhi's 1945 (1951, 2001) success using decades of nonviolent resistance like sit-ins, marches, and boycotts to negotiate Indian independence from British rule, and Martin Luther King, Jr.'s (1959) use of nonviolent active resistance like boycotts and labor strikes to create leverage for the poor and People of Color over the socioeconomically and racially privileged, and, most importantly, to stand for civil rights.

During the 1960s, grassroots citizen movements made public both diversity and the discrimination inappropriately based on that diversity. The Vietnam antiwar movement was in the forefront. In California, Hispanic farm workers organized for equitable treatment. Further, to resist subjugation, injustice, and patriarchal power, women's groups employed the model used in the Civil Rights movement. Students, environmentalists, Native peoples, and a range of groups around the globe took up the model of nonviolent action to address their own issues of justice and equity. While justice was not always the result, power blocks were challenged, and even eliminated in a few cases, especially through legislation designed to facilitate justice and equity for women and People of Color. Diverse citizens found that in engaging in disciplined, coercive nonviolent action, it is possible to be involved and have influence over policy making and implementation.

There were those who were disturbed by the successes of citizens movements and were threatened even by talk of equity for People of Color, women, indigenous groups, the linguistically diverse, or the poor. A backlash emerged that perpetuated a discourse of resentment, as well as reinscriptions of patriarchy and racism. Those who stood for diversity, justice, and equity were labeled as perpetuating "moral decay" (Berry, 1997, p. 35) as ideologies like feminism were put forward as evil and threats to the family. However, even as backlashes against perspectives like feminism emerged, a range of academic and community workers continued to stand for justice and equity, as demonstrated in the chapters of this book. Further, currently, some even acknowledge that justice for all human beings, even those who have been traditionally marginalized, may necessitate justice for other living creatures as well as the environment. These intersectional acknowledgements can result in expanded possibilities for collaborations and actions leading to increased justice broadly. The following are a reflection of the types of resources that can be used, or even generated, by researchers as they attempt to counter unjust power through nonviolent actions.

Example Ideas

Kaufman, C. (2003). *Ideas for action: Relevant theory for radical change.* Cambridge, MA: South End Press.

> Working as an activist since 1980, as well as an academic who served as the chairperson of a Women's Studies department, Cynthia Kaufman dedicates this volume to the people with whom she has worked through Students for Justice. As Howard Zinn notes on the cover endorsement, the text moves back and forth from theory to the construction of solutions for immediate problems as the complex entanglements of capitalism, racism, and oppression are discussed. The final two chapters focus on the range of possibilities for political action, including, as examples, ways to apply pressure on political systems that are not violent and coalition work on the streets.

Example Websites

Greshko, M., Parker, L., & Howard, B.C. (2018). A running list of how Trump is changing the environment. Retrieved from https://news.nationalgeographic.com/2017/03/how-trump-is-changing-science-environment/

Zinn Education Project. Retrieved from https://zinnedproject.org

> People's history project in collaboration with Rethinking Schools and Teaching for Change. Information regarding workshops and teaching materials that can be downloaded are included, ranging from "Know Your Rights Camp" by Colin Kaepernick, designed to take people's history to high school youth, to "teaching lessons" like a first-grade lesson in exploring women's rights through the 1908 textile strike.

The following are examples of some of the less-well-known activist groups:

Alley Cat Allies. The purpose of the organization is to protect the lives of cats through TNR (Trap, Neuter, Release) and it is expert in dealing with cat communities. Human community action projects locally around the globe are common. 7920 Norfolk Ave., Suite 600, Bethesda, MD 20814. Website: https://www.alleycat.org

Earthjustice Quarterly Magazine. The magazine is a publication of the nonprofit environmental law organization Earthjustice that creates partnerships to protect health, preserve wildlife, and combat climate change. "We exist because the earth needs a good lawyer." 50 California St., Suite 500, San Francisco, CA 94111. Website: https://earthjustice.org

Farm Sanctuary. Founded in 1986, the organization is an animal protection group that was the first shelter for farm animals in the United States. P.O. Box 150, Watkins Glen, New York, NY 14891. Website: https://farmsanctuary.org

National Anti-Vivisection Society. (2018). The life of a research dog. *ANIMALACTION.* 6–9. The organization is dedicated to ending the exploitation of animals used in science, to advancing science without harming animals. 53 W. Jackson Blvd., Suite 1552, Chicago, IL 60604. Website: https://www.NAVS.org

Peaceful Valley Donkey Rescue. This nonprofit is the largest donkey rescue in the United States, with 24 sanctuaries and 26 adoption centers around the country. 8317 Duckworth Rd., San Angelo, TX 76905. Website: www.donkeyrescue.org

Academic References

Berry, J.M. (1997). *The interest group society.* New York, NY: Addison Wesley Longman.

Droogendyk, L., Wright, S.C., Lubensky, M., & Winnifred, R.L. (2016). Acting in solidarity: Cross-group contact between disadvantaged group members and advantaged group allies. *Journal of Social Issues, 72*(2), 315–334.

Foucault, M. (2001). *Michel Foucault: Fearless speech*. J. Pearson, trans. Los Angeles, CA: Semiotext(e).

Gandhi, M.K. (2001). *Nonviolent resistance (satyagraha)*. New York, NY: Dover. (Originally published 1951)

Hannam, J. (2005). International dimensions of women's suffrage: At the crossroads of several interlocking identities. *Women's History Review, 14*(3–4), 543–560.

INCITE! (2009). *The revolution will not be funded* (1st ed.). New York, NY: South End Press.

King, M.L. (1959, July). *My trip to the land of Gandhi*. The Martin Luther King Papers Project. Retrieved from Kingencyclopedia.stanford.edu/primarydocuments/Vol5/July1959_MyTriptotheLandofGandhi.pdf

Long, J. (2013). Sense of place and place-based activism in the neoliberal city. *City, 17*(1), 52–67.

Pankhurst, E. (2007, April 27). Great speeches of the 20th century: Emmeline Pankhurst's freedom or death. *The Guardian*. Retrieved from https://www..theguardian.com/theguardian/2007/greatspeeches (Speech originally delivered in Hartford, CT, November 13, 1913)

Smeltzer, S., & Shade, L.R. (2017). Special Issue: Activism and communication scholarship in Canada. *Canadian Journal of Communication, 42*(1).

Children's Literature (activist beginnings)

Clinton, C. (2017). *She persisted: 13 American women who changed the world*. New York, NY: Philomel Books.

Harrison, V. (2017). *Little leaders: Bold women in Black history*. New York, NY: Little, Brown.

Levinson, C. (2017). *The youngest marcher: The story of Audrey Faye Hendricks, a young civil rights activist*. New York, NY: Atheneum Books.

Levy, D. (2016). *I dissent: Ruth Bader Ginsburg makes her mark*. New York, NY: Simon & Schuster.

Obama, B. (2010). *Of thee I sing: A letter to my daughters*. New York, NY: Alfred A Knopf.

Yousafzai, M. (2017). *Malala's magic pencil*. New York, NY: Little, Brown.

Infant Board Books

Nagara, I. (2013). *A is for activist*. New York, NY: Seven Stories Press.

Nagara, I. (2015). *Counting on community*. New York, NY: Seven Stories Press.

Using Critical Research Perspectives to Inform Nonviolent Resistance

The following resources are provided to supply the reader with examples from various critical theoretical perspectives, poststructuralism, and postmodern critical understandings like critical pedagogy, feminisms, queer theory, postcolonialism/subaltern/indigenous studies, critical race theory, and posthuman/postanthropocentric/feminist new materialist perspectives. The reader is reminded that all in some way ask the questions: Who/what is privileged/benefited/brought to the center? Who/what is marginalized/harmed/disqualified, even erased? Although not always philosophically aligned, each perspective in one way or the other addresses power, justice, and equity. Please note that the listing does not represent any particular order of importance or categorical labeling—it is just represented alphabetically. Additionally, most critical perspectives intersect with, critique, influence, and even becomewith other critical views. Therefore, the references are listed together, entangled within webs of possibilities to be generated by the reader. Finally, the authors are listed as starting points for beginning explorations. The reader may want to pursue further the work of a particular author.

Critical Research References and Example Investigations

Anzaldúa, G. (1999). *Borderlands—La frontera: The new mestiza*. San Francisco, CA: Aunt Lute Books.

Appiah, K. (1992). *In my father's house: Africa in the philosophy of culture*. London, England: Methuen.

Bacchi, C. (2017). Drug problematizations and politics: Deploying a poststructural analytic strategy. *Contemporary Drug Problems, 45*(1), 3–14.

Barad, K. (2003). Posthumanist performativity: Toward an understanding of how matter comes to matter. *Signs: Journal of Women in Culture and Society, 28*, 801–831.

Battiste, M. (2013). *Decolonizing education: Nourishing the learning spirit*. Vancouver, BC, Canada: UBC Press.

Battiste, M. (2000). (Ed.). *Reclaiming indigenous voice and vision*. Vancouver, BC, Canada: UBC Press.

Braidotti, R. (2013). *The posthuman*. Cambridge, England: Polity Press.

Burman, E. (1994). *Deconstructing developmental psychology*. New York, NY: Routledge.

Butler, J. (1992). Contingent foundations: Feminism and the question of "postmodernism." In J. Butler & J.W. Scott (Eds.), *Feminists theorize the political* (pp. 3–21). New York, NY: Routledge.

Cannella, G.S. (1997). *Deconstructing early childhood education: Social justice and revolution.* New York, NY: Peter Lang.

Cannella, G.S., & Viruru, R. (2004). *Childhood and postcolonizatiion: Power, education, and contemporary practice.* New York, NY: RoutledgeFalmer.

Chrulew, M., & Wadiwel, D.J. (2017). (Eds.). *Foucault and animals.* Leiden, Netherlands: Brill.

Coleman, R., & Ringrose, J. (2013). *Deleuze and research methodologies.* Edinburgh, Scotland: Edinburgh University Press.

Collins, P.H. (1990). *Black feminist thought: Knowledge, consciousness, and the politics of empowerment.* New York, NY: Routledge.

Crenshaw, K., Gotanda, N., Peller, G., & Thomas, K. (Eds.). (1995). *Critical race theory: The key writings that formed the movement.* New York, NY: The New Press.

Crilley, R., & Chatterje-Doody, P. (2018). Security studies in the age of "posttruth" politics: In defense of postructuralism. *Critical Studies in Security.* doi:10.1080/21624887.2018.1441634

Davies, B. (1993). *Shards of glass: Children reading and writing beyond gendered identities.* North Sydney, NSW, Australia: Allen & Unwin.

Deleuze, G., & Guattari, F. (1987). *A thousand plateaus: Capitalism and schizophrenia.* B. Massumi, trans. London, England: Athlone.

Denzin, N.K., Lincoln, Y.S., & Tuhwai Smith, L. (Eds.). (2008). *Handbook of critical indigenous methodologies.* London: SAGE.

Derrida, J. (1976). *Of grammatology.* Gayatri Chakravorty Spivak, trans. Baltimore, MD: The Johns Hopkins University Press. (Originally published in French, 1967)

Fanon, F. (2004). *The wretched of the earth.* R. Philcox, trans. New York, NY: Grove Press. (Originally published 1963)

Fletcher A.J. (2018). More than women and men: A framework for gender and intersectionality research on environmental crisis and conflict. In C. Fröhlich, G. Gioli, R. Cremades, & H. Myrttinen (Eds.), *Water security across the gender divide: Water security in a new world* (pp. 35–58). Dordrecht Springer.

Foucault, M. (1978). *The history of sexuality: An introduction,* Volume 1. Robert Hurley, trans. New York, NY: Pantheon.

Foucault, M. (1977). *Discipline and punish: The birth of the prison.* Alan Sheridan, trans. New York, NY: Vintage Books.

Gandhi, L. (1998). *Postcolonial theory: A critical introduction.* New York, NY: Columbia University Press.

Giraud, E., & Grove, S. (2013). Posthuman politics under biocapitalism. New Left Project: Philosophy and Theory. http://www.newleftproject.org/index.php/site/categories/C22

Grosz, E. (1994). *Volatile bodies: Towards a corporeal feminism*. Bloomington, IN: Indiana University Press.

Grumet, M.R. (1988). *Bitter milk: Women and teaching*. Amherst, MA: University of Massachusetts Press.

Haraway, D.J. (2016). *Staying with the trouble*. Durham, NC: Duke University Press.

Haraway, D.J. (2007). *When species meet*. Minneapolis, MN: University of Minnesota Press.

Haraway, D.J. (1992). *Primate visions: Gender, race, and nature in the world of modern science*. London, England: Verso.

Hodgson, N., & Standish, P. (2009). Uses and misuses of poststructuralism in educational research. *International Journal of Research & Method in Education, 32*(3), 309–326.

Holmes, D., & Gagnon, M. (2018). Power, discourse, and resistance: Poststructuralist influence in nursing. *Nursing Philosophy*. 2018.19:e.12200 doi:10.1111/nup.12200

hooks, b. (1984). *Feminist theory from margin to center*. Boston, MA: South End Press.

hooks, b. (1990). The politics of radical Black subjectivity. In *Yearning: Race, gender, and cultural politics* (pp. 15–22). Boston, MA: South End Press.

Huckaby, F. (2018). *Researching resistance: Public education after neoliberalism*. Gorham, ME: Myers Education Press.

Jones, R.C. (2015). Animal rights is a social justice issue. *Contemporary Justice Review, 4*, 467–482.

Koro-Ljungberg, M. (2016). *Reconceptualizing qualitative research*. Thousand Oaks, CA: SAGE.

Kovach, M. (2009). *Indigenous methodologies: Characteristics, conversations and contexts*. Toronto, Canada: University of Toronto Press.

Kristeva, J. (1986). *The Kristeva reader*. New York, NY: Columbia University Press.

Lather, P., & St. Pierre, E. A. (2013). Post qualitative research. *International Journal of Qualitative Studies in Education, 26*, 629–633.

Lerner, G. (1993). *The creation of feminist consciousness: From the middle ages to eighteen-seventy*. New York, NY: Oxford University Press.

Love, G. (2017). Towards a poststructural understanding of abortion and social class in England. *Global Public Health, 13*(6), 754–764. doi:10.1080/17441692.2017.1337798

MacClure, M. (2013). Researching without representation? Language and materiality in post-qualitative methodology. *International Journal of Qualitative Studies in Education, 26*, 658–667.

Matsuda, M., Lawrence, C., Delgado, R., & Crenshaw, I. (1993). *Words that wound: Critical race theory, assaultive speech, and the first amendment*. Boulder, CO: Westview.

Meissner, H. (2016). Conversing with the unexpected: Towards a feminist ethics of knowing. *Rhizomes: Cultural studies in emerging knowledge, 30*. Retrieved from http://www.rhizomes.net/issue30/meissner.html

Merchant, C. (1990). *The death of nature: Women, ecology and the scientific revolution*. New York, NY: Harper Collins.

Patel, L. (2016). *Decolonizing educational research: From ownership to answerability.* New York, NY: Routledge.

Papadopoulos, D. (2010). Insurgent posthumanism. *Ephemera: Theory & Politics of Organization, 10*(2), 134–151.

Said, E. (1978). *Orientalism.* New York, NY: Pantheon Press.

Sedgwick, E.K. (1993). *Tendencies.* Durham, NC: Duke University Press.

Sedgwick, E.K. (1990). *Epistemology of the closet.* New York, NY: Columbia University Press.

Sedgwick, E.K. (1985). *Between men: English literature and male homosocial desire.* New York, NY: Columbia University Press.

Shotwell, A. (2016). *Against purity: Living ethically in compromised times.* Minneapolis, MN: University of Minnesota Press.

Silin, J. (1995). *Sex, death, and the education of children: Our passion for ignorance in the age of AIDS.* New York, NY: Teachers College Press.

Solórzano, D. (1997). Images and words that wound: Critical race theory, racial stereotyping, and teacher education. *Teacher Education Quarterly, 24,* 5–19.

Spivak, G.C. (1993, 2009). *Outside the teaching machine.* New York, NY: Routledge.

Spivak, G.C. (1990, 2014). *The postcolonial critic: Interviews, strategies, dialogues.* New York, NY: Routledge.

St. Pierre, E.A., Jackson, A., & Mazzei, L. A. (2016). New empiricisms and new-materialisms. *Cultural Studies <=> Critical Methodologies, 16,* 99–110.

Steinberg, S., & Cannella, G.S. (Eds.). (2012). *Critical qualitative research reader.* New York, NY: Peter Lang.

Taguchi, H. L. (2013) Images of thinking in feminist materialisms: Ontological divergences and the production of researcher subjectivities. *International Journal of Qualitative Studies in Education, 26*(6), 706–716.

Tuck, E. (2009). Suspending damage: A letter to communities. *Harvard Educational Review, 79*(3), 409–428.

Tuhiwai Smith, L. (1999, 2012). *Decolonizing methodologies: Research and indigenous peoples.* London, England: Zed Books Ltd.

Ulmer, J.B. (2017). Posthumanism as research methodology: Inquiry in the Anthropocene. *International Journal of Qualitative Studies in Education, 30*(9), 832–838.

Viruru, R. (2001). *Decolonizing early childhood education: An Indian perspective.* New Delhi, India: SAGE.

Walkerdine, V. (1988). *The mastery of reason: Cognitive development and the production of rationality.* London, England: Routledge.

Weisberg, Z. (2009). The broken promises of monsters: Haraway, animals, and the humanist legacy. *Journal for Critical Animal Studies, 7*(2), 21–61.

Wolfe, C. (2012). *Before the law: Humans and other animals in a biopolitical frame.* Chicago, IL: University of Chicago Press.

Wolfe, C. (2010). *What is posthumanism?* Minneapolis, MN: University of Minnesota Press.

Wolfe, C. (2003). (Ed.). *Zoontologies*. Minneapolis, MN: University of Minnesota Press.
Yosso, T., Villalpando, O., Delgado Bernal, D., & Solórzano, D.G. (2001). *Critical race theory in Chicana/o education*. Paper presented at the National Association for Chicana and Chicano Studies Annual Conference, Paper 9. Retrieved from http://scholarworks.sjsu.edu/naccs/2001/Proceedings/9

Editors

Gaile S. Cannella (EdD, University of Georgia) is an independent scholar who has served as a tenured full professor at Texas A&M University–College Station and at Arizona State University–Tempe, as well as the Velma Schmidt Endowed Chair of Education at the University of North Texas. Her doctoral students have received outstanding dissertation awards from the American Educational Research Association. Dr. Cannella's scholarship focuses on diverse constructions of critical qualitative inquiry, reconceptualist childhood studies and education, and justice broadly, including related to environmental studies and the more-than-human. Dr. Cannella's work has appeared in a range of journals and volumes, including *Qualitative Inquiry, Cultural Studies <=> Critical Methodologies,* and *International Review of Qualitative Research.* Her most recent books are *Critical Qualitative Research Reader* (Peter Lang, 2012) with Shirley Steinberg; *Reconceptualizing Early Childhood Care and Education* (Peter Lang, 2014, 2nd edition 2018) with Marianne Bloch and Beth Swadener; *Critical Qualitative Inquiry: Foundations and Futures* (Left Coast Press, 2015) with Michelle Pérez and Penny Pasque; and *Critical Examinations of Quality in Childhood Education and Care* (Peter Lang, 2016) with Michelle Pérez and I-Fang Lee. She is currently working on research projects that include early years critical perspectives in education, and critical qualitative inquiry as public activisms and unthought imaginary. Dr. Cannella received the 2017 Reconceptualizing Early Childhood Education and Care Bloch Career Award.

Yvonna S. Lincoln received her Ed.D. in Higher Education from Indiana University in 1977. Dr. Lincoln joined the Educational Administration and Human Resource Development Department at Texas A&M as a Professor in 1991. She teaches graduate courses in qualitative research methods, the foundations of American higher education, proposal preparation and organizational theory. Her research focuses on neoliberal and corporatization shifts in faculty worklife and university administration, and also in the development of qualitative methods. She is the co-editor of *Qualitative Inquiry Journal,* and serves on several other editorial boards. She has written over 100 peer-reviewed journal articles and chapters, and written, edited or co-edited more than a dozen books, She has chaired over 100 doctoral committees, and served on many more. She won the Presidential Citation from the American Educational Research Association in 2013.

Contributors

M. Francyne Huckaby is Professor of Curriculum Studies and core faculty of Women and Gender Studies, Africana and African American Studies, and Comparative Race and Ethnic Studies at Texas Christian University. Her scholarship on community organizing and resistance to neoliberal education reform puts filmmaking to work as a form of inquiry and making public—publicaré—research and sites of resistance and struggle. Her publications include *Researching Resistance: Public Education after Neoliberalism* and *Making Research Public in Troubled Times: Pedagogy, Activism, and Critical Obligations*.

Valerie Kinloch is the Renée and Richard Goldman Dean of the School of Education and Professor at the University of Pittsburgh. Her scholarship examines the literacies and community engagements of youth and adults inside and outside schools. Author of publications on race, place, literacy, and equity, her books include: *June Jordan: Her Life and Letters*, *Harlem On Our Minds: Place, Race, and the Literacies of Urban Youth* and, among others, *Crossing Boundaries: Teaching and Learning with Urban Youth*. Her book, *Harlem On Our Minds*, received the Outstanding Book of the Year Award from the American Educational Research Association, and *Crossing Boundaries* was a staff pick for professional development by the Teaching Tolerance Education Magazine. She received her undergraduate degree from Johnson C. Smith University in Charlotte, NC, and her graduate degrees from Wayne State University in Detroit, MI.

Janet L. Miller is Professor in the Department of Arts & Humanities-English & Education at Teachers College, Columbia University, as well as Faculty-At-Large, Columbia University. She served as Founding Managing Editor, from 1978 through 1998, of *JCT: The Journal of Curriculum Theorizing* and as Director of its Bergamo Annual Conference on Curriculum Theory and Classroom Practice. The author of many journal articles and book chapters that entangle curriculum, feminist and qualitative research theorizings and studies, Miller's work includes *Maxine Greene and Education* and *Curriculum and Collaboration: Communities without Consensus*. Other single-authored books include *Sounds of Silence Breaking: Women, Autobiography, Curriculum*, and *Creating Spaces and Finding Voices: Teachers Collaborating for Empowerment*, which received both the Stessin Prize for Outstanding Faculty Scholarly Publication and the James N. Britton Award for Inquiry from the National Council of Teachers of English. As well, Miller co-edited, with William Ayers, *A Light in Dark Times: Maxine Greene and the Unfinished Conversation*.

Index

"breaking with tradition", 44, 53
"Gold Star" mother, 71
#Me Too, 73, 81
#Say Her Name, 73, 81
#Time's Up, 73, 81
2016 U.S presidential election, 1, 4, 19, 45, 50, 52, 71-73, 97, 103, 112
    debates, 17

A
aboriginal, 108
activism, 2, 17, 49, 50, 69, 112, 115, 117-119, 121, 123, 125, 126
Albright, Madeleine, 83, 84, 95
American Educational Research Association, 17 25, 51, 95, 125, 126
American(s), 10, 18, 35, 43, 47, 50, 54, 71, 103, 104, 107, 109, 118
ancestor(s), 27, 30, 53
Anthony, Susan B., 71, 99, 110
anticolonial science, 16, 17, 22, 112
Atwood, Margaret, 20, 21, 23, 85, 86, 89, 92, 95
autoethnography, 4, 17
    also see ethnography

B
Baldwin, James, 52, 54, 55
Baudrillard, Jean, 26, 40
becomewith, 10, 97, 98, 105, 106, 119
    becomingwith, 1, 105
    becomingswith, 97, 107, 115
biodiversity, 59
Black feminist thought, 18, 49, 50, 55, 83, 120
Black, Woman, and Transgressive (BWT), 18, 19, 43-46, 49-52, 55, 56
Bland, Sandra, 47
Bridges, Ruby, 99, 109
Butler, Judith, 20, 21, 74, 77, 78, 83, 87-89, 92, 93, 120

C
capitalist patriarchy, 1-3, 44, 52
    whitelash, 2, 18, 52
capitalocene, 3, 23, 105
Carey, Miriam, 46, 47, 55
case study, 12
children, 3, 4, 36, 44, 46, 48, 55, 67, 85, 86, 93, 111, 118, 120, 122
Chisholm, Shirley Anita St. Hill, 19, 22, 43-46, 48, 50, 52, 54-56
Chronicle of Higher Education, 57, 68, 69
citizen(s), 18, 29, 43, 67, 71, 89, 107, 109, 115, 116
    of the world, 34, 37
civil rights, 4, 15, 51, 73, 87, 103, 109, 115, 118
Clinton, Hillary Rodham, 17, 21, 50-54, 71, 73, 80, 82-84, 92, 94, 95, 97, 100, 109, 111, 112, 118
coalition building, 2, 88, 108, 116
Congressional Black Caucus, 43
conventional inquiry, 6, 9, 11, 80
Cox, Lavern, 99, 109
Crenshaw, Kimberle, 2, 22, 87, 93, 120, 121
critical
    analysis, 81
    animal studies, 122
    cartographies, 79
    criticalist, 15
    humanities, 76
    inquiry, 4, 6, 9, 16, 20, 23, 73, 81, 107, 112, 119, 120
    justice, 5, 7
    pedagogy, 15, 40, 94, 119
    posthumanities, 76, 78, 92
    qualitative inquiry (research), 4-6, 16-19, 23, 24, 51, 72-74, 76, 80-82, 90, 91, 93, 95, 96, 115, 122, 125
    race theory, 16, 119, 120, 122, 123
    realism(ist), 8, 11-13
    research, 1, 2, 7, 15, 16, 97, 106, 119

resistance, 92
scholars, 1, 2, 4, 6, 7, 15, 16, 20, 21
social science, 16, 21, 22
Critical Theory, 16, 23, 24
transformations, 6
critique, 5, 6, 14, 20, 22-24, 64, 73, 75, 77, 79-83, 85, 90, 91, 93, 95, 96, 119

D
data collection, 11,12
Davis, Angela, 52, 54, 55, 99, 110
death, 18, 21, 27, 33, 34, 47, 118, 121, 122
Deleuze, Giles13, 22, 60, 68, 120
democracy, 33, 58
design, 8, 11, 12, 20, 115, 117
desire, 20, 27, 33, 34, 36, 74, 80, 102, 122
Dillard, Cynthia, 30, 40
dream(s), 18, 25, 27, 28, 30, 36, 111
discrazure, 25

E
education, 1, 3, 4, 12, 14, 17, 20, 22, 24, 25, 40, 43, 44, 49, 51, 53, 55, 57-64, 66-69, 72, 73, 76, 81, 84, 90, 93, 96, 106, 112, 113, 117, 119, 123
Elder Marie Jones, 98, 106
elder(s), 27, 98, 106
enlightenment, 5, 6, 8, 102
entanglement(s), 8, 10, 20, 21, 77, 92, 108, 110, 116
environment(al), 3, 6, 17-19, 106, 107, 111, 116, 117, 120
  damage, 3
  destruction, 3
  justice, 3, 109
  protections, 59
  environmentalists, 71, 115
episteme(sui)cide, 34
epistemology(ical), 8-10, 13, 15, 39, 45, 49, 50, 68, 77, 81, 82, 122
equity, 1, 2, 4, 6, 9, 13, 15, 18, 21, 43, 45, 54, 66, 67, 115, 116, 119
  inequity, 1, 3, 16
eros, 25
erotic, 25, 26
ethic(s)(o), 9, 10, 15, 22, 40, 76, 79, 90, 121, 122
ethical responsibilities, 2, 5
ethnography, 12, 60, 63, 66, 69, 93
  also see autoethnography

F
farm workers,115
FEAS, Feminist Educators Against Sexism, 110, 113
feminist(ism), 1, 8, 15, 22, 40, 49, 50, 55, 73, 75, 78, 79, 82, 85, 87, 89, 90, 92-94, 96, 101, 104, 107, 108, 112, 113, 116, 119, 122

First Amendment, 57, 121
First Nations, 71, 99, 108
FiveThirtyEight.com, 26
Foucault, Michel, 3, 5, 6, 18, 22, 23, 26, 35, 40, 81, 94, 118, 120
freedom, 4, 32, 40, 45, 47, 49, 61, 102, 118

G
Gandhi, Mahatma, 115, 118, 120
gender(ed), 2, 6, 16, 19, 20, 25, 40, 43, 44, 52, 54, 65, 72, 74, 79, 81-84, 86, 87, 92-94, 100, 102, 120, 121
grounded theory, 12, 23, 24
Guattari, Felix, 13, 22, 60, 68, 120
Guba, Egon, 9, 10, 14, 23, 24, 60, 68, 69, 75, 94

H
Hamer, Fannie Lou, 19, 45
Haraway, Donna, 1, 17, 23, 87, 88, 90, 91, 94, 97, 107, 112, 121, 122
higher education, 4, 22, 57, 61-64, 66-69
human(s), 1, 3, 6, 7, 10, 12, 15, 16, 18, 23, 39, 46, 48, 53, 73, 76, 78-81, 83, 88, 95, 97, 106, 107, 117, 122
  beings, 2, 3, 5-7, 10, 14, 15, 17, 45, 116
  dehumanization(ing), 46,50,83
  humane, inhuman, inhumane, 59, 76, 88
  humanity, 19, 31, 37, 43, 46, 49, 52, 79
  more-than-human, 1, 7, 107, 111
  nonhuman, 3, 7, 16, 76, 81, 88
  other-than-human animals, 106
  privilege, 6, 7, 9, 107
  rights, 19, 20, 43, 44, 51, 74, 86, 103, 111, 113
  also see posthuman

I
identity(ies), 2, 19, 20, 23, 43, 44, 46, 52, 54, 71, 73-77, 79, 81, 83, 87, 89, 92, 93, 102, 105, 108, 112, 118, 120
  politics, 2, 19, 20, 44, 46, 74, 89, 104, 105
  rights, 19, 44
immigrant(s), 29, 72, 103, 105, 108
indigenous, 15, 16, 22, 24, 80, 99, 106, 107, 112, 113, 116, 119, 122
injustice, 1-4, 15, 17, 44, 97, 99, 106, 115
  also see justice
International Congress of Qualitative Inquiry, 17, 69
intersectional, 1, 4, 21, 98, 99, 102, 104, 106, 110, 112, 116
intersectionality(ies), 2, 87, 106, 107, 112, 120

Index

J
Jim Crow, 73, 92
Jordon, June, 19, 45
justice, 1-9, 13, 15-22, 35, 39, 43, 46, 49, 54, 58, 68, 69, 75, 93, 103, 106, 108, 110, 111, 115-117, 119-121
    also see injustice

K
King Jr., Martin Luther, 1, 23, 115, 118
King, Coretta Scott, 108, 109, 112

L
LaDuke, Winona, 99, 109
law, 11, 27, 40, 87, 100-102, 111, 117, 122
line(s) of flight, 13
Lorde, Audre, 5, 18, 19, 23, 25, 28, 31, 34, 40, 45, 87, 95, 104, 105, 111, 112
love, 18, 23, 25, 27, 34, 39, 50, 52, 55, 101, 106
Lyles, Charleena, 48

M
McConnell, Mitch, 99, 108, 109
McCray, Antron, 35
methodology(ical), 2, 9-11, 18, 19, 22-24, 45, 63, 68, 75, 94-96, 112, 113, 120-122
misogyny(ous), 1-3, 20, 21, 27, 44, 51, 53, 71-73, 80, 82, 86, 89, 98, 99, 101, 103, 105, 108, 110, 112, 113
modern(ist)(ism), 5, 8, 13, 14, 16, 22, 68, 69, 108, 121
Moore, Michael, 102
more-than-human, 1, 7, 107, 111
    also see human
movements, 23, 46, 74, 81, 85, 86, 115, 116, 120
    #Me Too, 81, 85, 86
    American Indian, 103
    Black Lives Matter, 46, 47, 73, 103
    Civil Rights, 73, 115, 103
    LBGTQ Liberation, 110
    Never Again, 73
    Women's, 73, 87
Muslim, 71, 72, 103, 105

N
nasty women, 17, 51, 71, 100, 111
National Science Foundation, 57
nationalism, 27
Navajo, 98, 106
Neoliberalism, 3, 19, 22, 27, 59, 60, 108, 118, 121
new materialism, 16, 76, 77, 95, 96, 122
news, 20, 29, 30, 36, 38, 47, 55, 57, 66, 71, 86, 113, 117
nonviolent(ce), 1, 4, 17, 18, 21, 51, 80, 90, 92, 98, 115, 116, 118, 119
    also see violence

O
Obama, Barack H., 53, 57, 84, 89, 92, 100, 103, 118
Omar, Ilhan, 99, 109
ontology(ical), 8-11, 13, 14, 62, 68, 75, 77, 79, 81, 83, 94, 96, 122

P
pacifist, 31, 33, 34
Parks, Rosa, 99, 109
patriarchy(cal), 1-3, 20, 23, 24, 44, 50, 52, 54, 86, 95, 97, 98, 100, 101, 102, 104, 105, 110, 116
    capitalism, 1, 18, 51, 52
    capitalocene, 105
    households, 101
    power, 115
    social order, 101
    whitelash, 17, 51, 52
People of Color, 3, 7, 44, 46, 48, 103, 105, 106, 115, 116
performance(s), 2, 4, 5, 8, 11, 15, 17, 20, 97, 98
performativity, 77, 119
pessimism, 30, 31
poetry, 27, 28
policy, 36, 58, 59, 62, 65-67, 112, 113, 116
positivist(ism), 5, 91, 95
postanthropocentric (ism), 10, 91, 119
postcolonial(ism), 1, 15, 16, 18, 24, 75, 77, 79, 89, 94, 99, 107, 108, 119, 120, 122
posthuman, 8, 15, 16, 20, 76-79, 81, 89, 92, 94, 95, 107, 113, 119, 120, 122
    inquiry, 10
postmodern, 8, 11, 14-16, 22-24, 34, 36, 64, 68, 75, 76, 94, 119
    postmodern(ist) (ism), 14, 22, 34, 94, 120
postpositive(ism)(ist), 8, 10-14
poststructural(ism), 1, 8, 15-18, 20, 75-78, 89, 94, 96, 119, 121
post-truth, 34, 36, 120
power, 1-9, 13, 15, 16, 25, 26, 31, 34, 36, 40, 41, 44, 49-52, 54, 55, 63, 67, 72, 84, 86-88, 91, 93, 95, 99, 101, 107, 109, 111, 115, 116, 119, 120, 121
protest, 2, 19, 20, 36, 39, 47, 52, 58, 68, 81, 89, 97, 106, 107, 109, 113
    protest performances, 2, 98

public, 1, 2, 19, 20, 37, 46, 58-61, 66, 88, 89, 115, 121
  action, 4, 97, 115
  activists, 2
  assaults, 47
  discourse, 34, 49
  dissemination, 4
  education/schools, 3, 51, 57, 95, 121
  ethnography, 66
  justice, 19
  opposition, 36
  scholarship, 115
Punjabi, 98, 106
Pussy Riot, 101, 102, 113

Q
qualitative research/inquiry, 4-13, 16-19, 21, 24, 51, 60, 61, 63, 66, 69, 72-77, 80, 82, 84, 90, 92-96, 112, 113, 115, 121, 122
queer theory, 15, 16, 119

R
race, 6, 16, 19, 20, 22, 23, 25, 40, 43, 52, 72, 74, 75, 79, 83, 84, 86, 87, 93, 94, 102, 112, 119, 120, 121-123
racism, 1-3, 21, 40, 45, 46, 51, 53-55, 73, 84, 89, 90, 97, 103, 105, 107, 108, 116
rallies, 29, 102
reality, 7-15, 34, 36, 45, 51, 52, 65, 85, 111
red dragon, 25
refugee(s), 71, 109
Republican National Convention, 107
resist(ance)(ing), 2, 4, 17-22, 26, 31, 39, 44, 45, 51, 52, 55, 59, 61, 67, 68, 75, 80, 82, 90, 92, 95, 97, 98, 108, 109, 111, 115, 116, 118, 119, 121
Richardson, Kevin, 35
Rivera, Sylvia, 99, 110
Russia, 84, 101, 113

S
Salaam, Yusef, 35
Santana, Raymond, 35
seduction, 26
Sessions, Jeff, 69, 108, 112
sexism, 3, 21, 85, 97, 112, 113
Shroeder, Patricia, 102
silence, 2, 10, 14, 18, 30, 31, 95, 104, 106, 126
social media, 60, 65, 83
Sojourner Truth, 2, 50
Soleimanpour, Nassim, 41
speciesism, 1, 3

spirit murder, 27
Spivak, Gayatri, 18, 87, 88, 91, 95, 120, 122
struggle, 1, 4, 5, 7, 20, 24, 31, 50, 52, 54, 60, 74, 83, 97, 103
suicide, 27, 34
survival, 2, 4, 18, 30, 34, 50, 79, 98, 105, 106, 110, 111, 113

T
theory, 8, 11, 12, 15, 16, 22, 24, 40, 45, 68, 69, 92, 93, 95, 96, 112, 116, 119-123
Tolokonnikova, Nadya, 102, 113
transgressive subjectivity, 19, 43, 44, 51
Trump, Donald J., 3, 17-19, 21, 24, 26, 29, 37-39, 71, 72, 84, 86, 88, 89, 92, 93, 97, 100, 102, 104, 105, 110, 112, 113, 117

U
undesignatable, 74, 89
unaccountable, 27
universal truth, 12, 14, 15

V
violence, 1, 3, 21, 29, 31, 39, 44-47, 51-54, 58, 72, 74, 79, 83, 89, 90, 92, 93, 101, 102, 107
  against Black girls and women, 45, 46, 49, 50, 51
  against Black boys and men, 52
  against Black love, 52
  against Communities of Color, 46
  against LGBTQIA+Communities, 46
  against children and their families, 46
  also see nonviolence
  also see children
vote(d)(ing), 27, 33, 39, 50, 53, 54, 71, 83, 86, 100

W
Warren, Elizabeth, 108, 109, 112, 113
warrior, 18, 25, 27, 31, 33, 34, 41, 106
White Rabbit, Red Rabbit, 41
white supremacy, 36, 104
whitelash, 2, 17, 18, 51, 52, 72, 73, 92, 95
whiteness, 72, 82
Wise, Korey, 35
woman, 18-20, 25, 29, 39, 40, 43-56, 65, 71, 73, 74, 76, 78, 80-89, 91, 92, 98, 100, 102-104, 106, 108, 109, 111, 113
Women's March, 72, 93, 103, 104, 112, 113,
Woodhull, Victoria, 102

Y
Yousafzai, Malala, 99, 110, 118